Topics and Questions in Needlework

K M Hartley and J M Roe

 *Heinemann Educational Books . London*

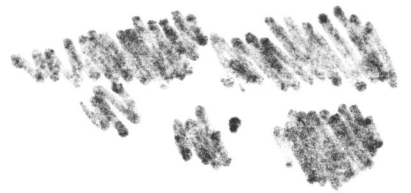

Heinemann Educational Books Ltd
22 Bedford Square, London WC1B 3HH

London Edinburgh Melbourne Auckland
Hong Kong Singapore Kuala Lumpur New Delhi
Ibadan Nairobi Johannesburg
Exeter(NH) Kingston Port of Spain

With Answers ISBN 0 435 42836 5
Text only ISBN 0 435 42835 7
© K. M. Hartley and J. M. Roe 1977
First published 1977
Reprinted 1978, 1979, 1982

Text set in 10/11 pt IBM Journal, printed by photolithography,
and bound in Great Britain by Spottiswoode Ballantyne Ltd.
Colchester and London

Preface

It is intended that this book be used mainly by students preparing for examinations in Needlework. The questions are on topics which have been chosen to cover a wide range of work common to the syllabuses of the major examining boards. It is hoped that the book may find a wider use as a source of questions for homework and revision and for classwork with students at pre-examination stages. It could also be used during the occasional staff absence and for classes with students of mixed ability. The questions are arranged in order of complexity.

The answers and marking schemes have been given in considerable detail based on our wide experience in examining, in the hope that both teachers and students may realize what is expected for detailed answers in an examination.

The style of the questions is similar to that of the short answer paper of several of the examining boards. While we realize that not all the examining boards use this system, the guidance provided in asking for a specific number of points will be of benefit to students answering essay-type questions.

We hope that you will find as much stimulation for your teaching in using the book as we have found in preparing it.

K.M.H.
J.M.R.

Acknowledgements

We are grateful to:-

The Local Examinations Syndicate, Cambridge, for allowing us to use past examination questions as a basis on which to work,

The Butterick Fashion Marketing Company, for allowing us to use illustrations from their catalogues and primers,

Our artist, Jane Lewington, who has worked very hard to clarify all the detail we required in diagrams and sketches,

Our publishers who have encouraged us every step of the way.

The authors express their appreciation of the help they have received during many years of teaching from the following books and periodicals: *Clothes*, M. Butler, Batsford. *Needlework for Schools*, M. Neal, Blackie. *Needlework*, R. Giles, Methuen. *Basic Needlework*, W. Bull, Longman. *Making Your Own Clothes*, V. Cliffe, Arnold. *Standard Processes in Dressmaking*, E. Lucy Towers, University of London Press. *Fashion Design Drawing*, P. J. Ireland, Batsford. *Dress Design*, B. Naylor, Batsford. *The Vogue Sewing Book*. *The Simplicity Sewing Book*.

Introduction

Each question in the book carries 50 marks and it is suggested that the questions should take about 20 minutes each when the student has become familiar with the type of question.

In those questions where the choice of fabric has been left to the student, only a general outline of the answer has been given, since it is impossible to give descriptions of all the fabrics which would be suitable.

Marking of fabric selection

type of fabric (1) giving fibre and fabric
description (3) giving method of construction, feel,
R.S. and W.S. appearance

    e.g. brushed nylon (1) knitted (1) W.S. smooth
           (1) R.S. soft and raised (1)
           cotton poplin (1) plain weave (1) R.S. and
           W.S. alike (1) lustrous (1)

Silhouettes are provided. These or similar ones should be used where required. Sketches of garments on examination scripts are frequently small and lacking in the necessary detail. Students should be encouraged to use the silhouettes properly. The outline of the figure should not be visible through the garment unless it would actually show (e.g. in transparent sleeves) and the detail on the garment must be accurate. The omission of centre back seams especially below zips, armhole seams, back neck openings in garments which are close fitting at the neck and not relating the front view to the back view are common faults.

Students should be encouraged to use abbreviations as they save time in writing and can be easily identified in written answers and diagrams when the work is being marked. Abbreviations used in this book are:

R.S.	right side	C.B.	centre back
W.S.	wrong side	S.G.	straight grain
F.L.	fitting line	cm	centimetre
S.A.	seam allowance	mm	millimetre
C.F.	centre front	xway	crossway
L.H.	left hand	R.H.	right hand

Questions 1-70

Question 1

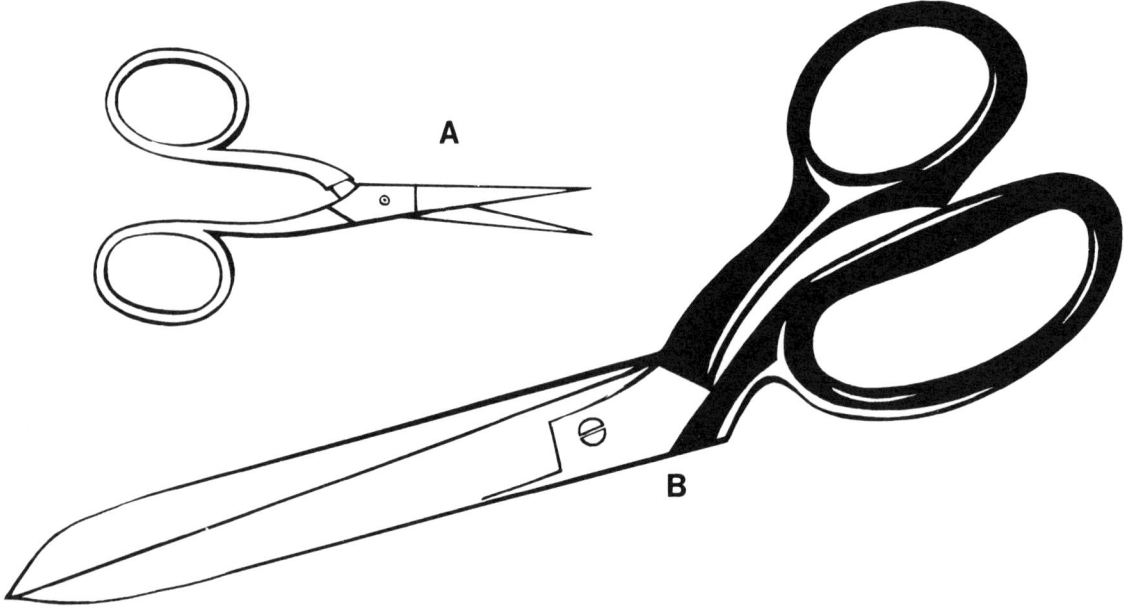

a. Give the correct names for the scissors illustrated. State the specific purpose for which each is designed.

b. Complete the following instructions to help a right-handed person use scissors B correctly.
Place your _____ in the small hole and _____ _____ in the _____ hole. The _____ blade should be _____ the fabric, _____ the table. Keep your _____ hand _____ on the fabric to hold it _____ while cutting. Use _____ cuts to ensure a _____ edge.

c. List five important points to consider when buying a new tape-measure.

d. Describe the following types of needle used in hand sewing. State the specific purpose of each type. (i) Sharps, (ii) Betweens, (iii) Crewel, (iv) Tapestry.

e. List five other items not mentioned above which should be included in your work basket. Give two uses for each item.

Question 2

a. What general name is given to the items illustrated?

b. Give the particular name for each of these items.

c. Give four general points to consider when deciding to use any of the above.

d. Suggest a suitable, but different, position for each of the items.

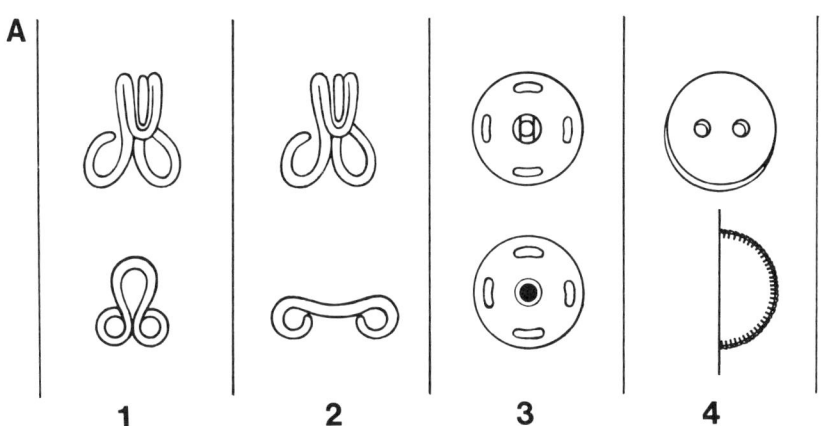

A

1   **2**   **3**   **4**

e. Diagrams B, C and D relate to item 4 in diagram A.

   (i) Explain the numbered arrows on diagram B to show that you understand the process fully.

   (ii) Write notes to describe how to complete the process using diagrams C and D to help you.

   (iii) This method can also be used to make a worked bar for a hook and for a belt loop. What are the subtle differences between them? Give a position where each could be placed.

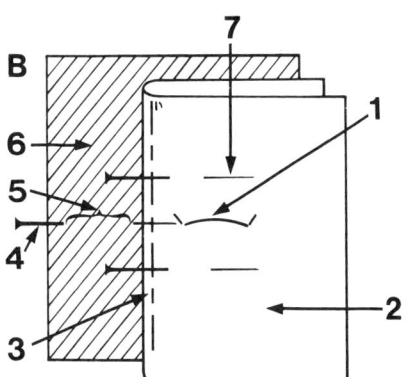

B

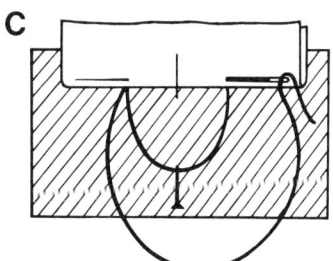

C

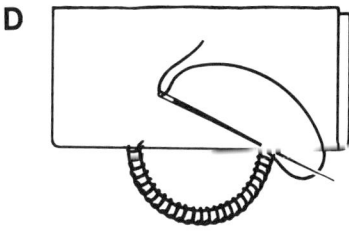

D

Question 3

Study the child's dress illustrated below.

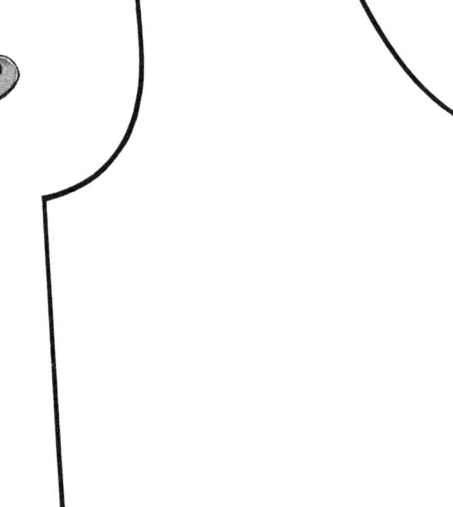

a. (i) Trace the pattern for the front bodice and on it mark: the fitting lines, dart, C.F. line, straight grain arrow, notch for the collar position, notches for matching to back bodice, button and buttonhole positions.

(ii) List the other pattern markings which would probably be on this pattern piece.

b. The armhole is bound. On your tracing shade in the area which will be cut off before binding commences. Why is this done?

4

c. Name three temporary stitches which could be used on this dress. Give two positions where each could be used.

d. It would be necessary to cut crossway strips to bind the armholes of this dress. For each of the diagrams below explain the numbered arrows.

e. (i) What is the usual width of a crossway strip?
(ii) What is the usual depth of the finish bind?
(iii) When joining the crossway strips into a circle for the armhole, where should the join be?
(iv) Name the stitch which is worked by hand to secure the binding on the W.S.
(v) What is the commercial form of crossway strips called?
(vi) Why does this dress need a side zip as well as the front opening?

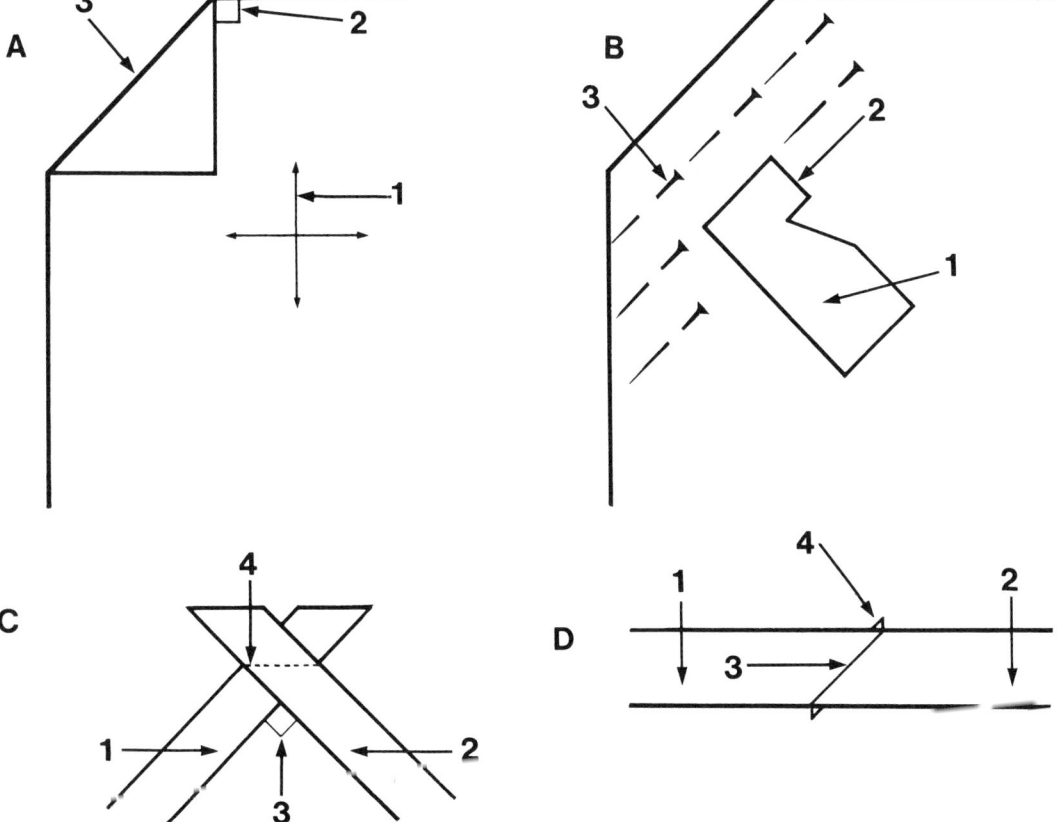

Question 4

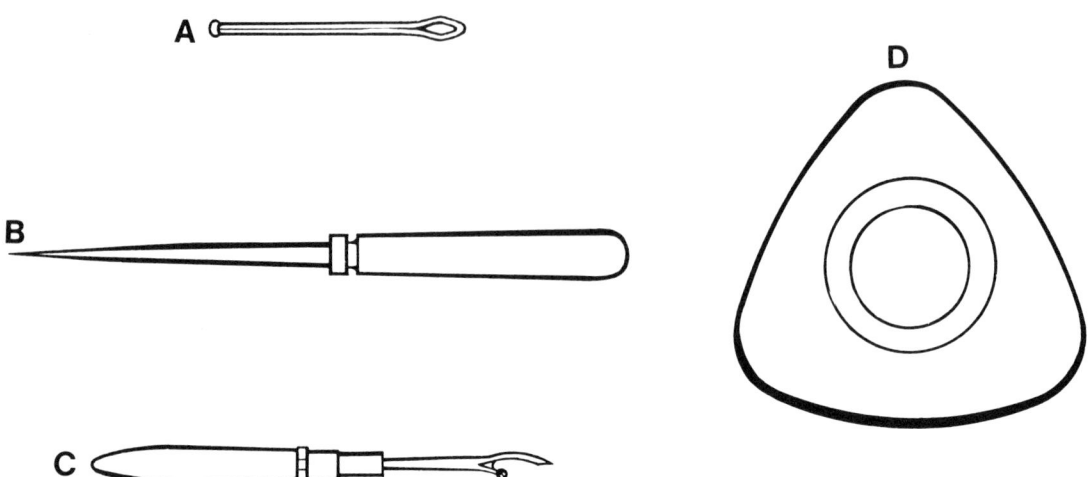

a. Name and describe each of the sewing aids illustrated. State why each is useful and give a specific example where each may be used.

b. What points would you consider when choosing:
    (i) a thimble, (ii) pins?

c. Explain briefly the advantages of wearing a thimble when you are sewing.

d. How could you make a useful measuring gauge? Explain its usefulness.

e. You have been promised a hem marker for a present. Describe the one you would like.

f. (i) Machine needles are available in several sizes. State three of these sizes and for each suggest two fabrics for which they would be suitable.
    (ii) What other points must be considered before commencing to machine on a garment?
    (iii) For which type of fabrics are ball point machine needles recommended?

Question 5

Select the odd one out in each of the following and state a reason in each case.

a. Sharps, Betweens, Crewel, Tapestry.
b. Sylko, Star, Drima, Gütermann.
c. Inverted, Knife, Box, Accordian.
d. Gathering, Gauging, Pleating, Easing.
e. Vandyke, Wave, French Knot, Honeycombe.
f. Stem, Chain, Wave, Cross.
g. Oversewing, Overcasting, Loop Stitch, Herringbone.
h. Eton, Sailor, Crew, Shawl.
i. Puffed, Raglan, Magyar, Kimono.
j. Turtle, Polo, Crew, Peter Pan.
k. Hedge-tear, Thin place, Household, Swiss.
l. Fitting line, Seam allowance, Seam line, Stitching line.
m. Raglan, Bishop, Set-in, Puff.
n. Princess, Empire, 'A', 'B'.
o. Back waist, Shoulder, Bust, Crutch.
p. Culottes, Bermudas, Pantaloons, Kilt.
q. Shoulder, Elbow, Waist, Hip.
r. Ankle, Mid-calf, Thigh, Knee.
s. Press studs, Hook and eye, Button, Velcro.
t. Lace, Ribbon, Rouleau, Tape.
u. Cummerbund, Sash, Halter, Belt.
v. Crutch, Inside leg, Outside leg, Back waist.
w. Notches, Fitting line, Balance mark, Cutting line.
x. Hips, Waist, Bust, Back waist.
y. Grain line, Fitting line, Place to fold, Cutting line.

Question 6

a. List six points to consider when purchasing an ironing board.
b. Certain garments and parts of garments are very difficult to press on an ironing board or on a table. Give five instances where the use of a sleeve board would make the task easier.
c. A pressing mitt is very useful. Explain how to use this when pressing a plain set-in sleeve head in a cotton poplin blouse.
d. Explain how to make an inexpensive seam roller.
e. (i) Name three fabrics of differing weight which could be used for pressing cloths.
    (ii) For each pressing cloth you have named state a fabric with which it could be used.
f. List ten points you should consider when buying a new steam iron.
g. Give words to complete the following sentences about the care and use of a steam iron.

Before using the iron check that the _____ is not cracked and that the _____ is not tangled or _____.
Make sure the plug is firmly in the _____ and fill the iron before _____ on. Use only _____ water as this prevents _____ building up inside the _____ plate.
Give the iron time to _____ before switching to steam.
Always rest the iron on its _____. After use, completely _____ the iron while warm and allow to _____ thoroughly standing on its _____ and _____ before putting away.

Question 7

Carbon paper and a tracing wheel are often useful for transferring pattern markings onto fabric.

a.　(i) Name four fabrics on which they can be used safely.

(ii) Giving reasons, name four fabrics on which they should not be used.

b.　Give words to complete the following instructions to explain the correct use of carbon paper and tracing wheel for marking a dart.

Place the fabric _____ together, with one sheet of _____ paper facing each _____ of the fabric and the pattern on the _____ . _____ securely in position, making sure that the _____ is in the same _____ as when cutting out. Using the _____ and a ruler, mark on the printed _____ being careful not to extend them beyond the _____ of the dart.

c.　The following diagrams show another method of transferring pattern markings. Name the method and explain the diagrams.

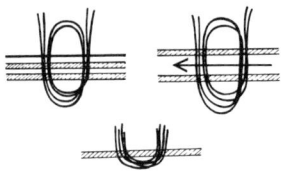

d.　Copy the diagrams of the three temporary stitches shown below. For each, name the stitch and draw the needle and thread in the correct position for forming the next stitch. Give two uses for each stitch.

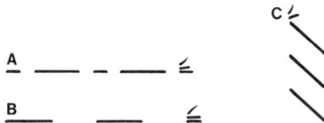

Question 8

a.   Trace the front and side view silhouettes which are on the inside back cover. On your drawings show by clearly labelled lines where each of the following body measurements should be taken:

(i) Front view: bust, waist, hip.

(ii) Side view: bust, back waist, outside leg.

b.   Give four general points to be observed when taking body measurements and detailed instructions for one of the measurements mentioned in (*a*).

c.   Which size of pattern do you use? Is this a Misses, Miss Petite or Young Teen pattern? If it is none of these, state which type it is. Give the corresponding measurements of this pattern size.

d.   If your body measurements do not correspond exactly to a pattern size, should you buy a pattern of the nearest bust or the nearest hip measurement? Give reasons for your answer.

e.   'Body measurements are the actual measurements of your body, they are not the measurements of the pattern.' Explain this statement giving your reasons.

f.   What make of pattern do you prefer? Give three reasons.

g.   Explain the following commercial descriptions of patterns:

(i) 'Wardrobe pattern',

(ii) 'Jiffy',

(iii) 'Easy to sew',

(iv) 'For knits only'.

h.   Ideally should you buy the pattern or the fabric first? Why is this not always practicable?

i.   What points should you consider when choosing a skirt pattern for yourself?

Question 9

a. The choice of seam for a garment depends on three factors. What are they?

b. Name the two seams illustrated below.

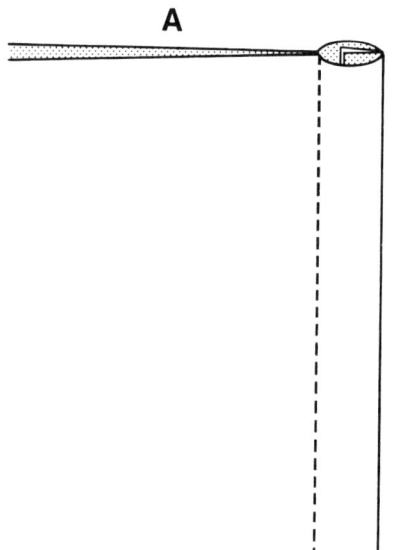

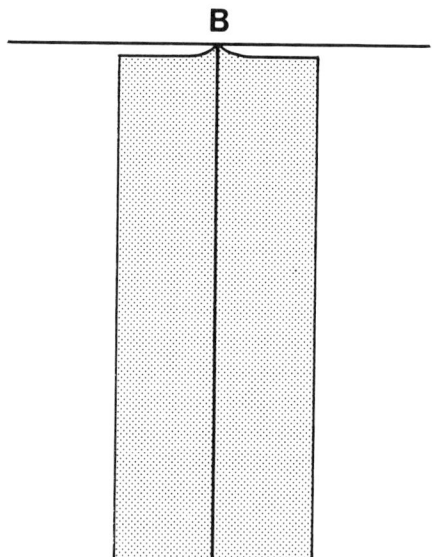

c. (i) Suggest two fabrics for which seam A would be suitable.
(ii) For each of these fabrics state a suitable garment and a position on the garment where the seam could be used.
(iii) Give two advantages of using this seam.

d. (i) Seam B practically always requires neatening. Draw diagrams to show six different methods of neatening this seam. Name each method and state a suitable fabric for each one (each fabric should be different). You may trace diagram B to help you with your answer.
(ii) State one fabric on which it may not be necessary to neaten the seam. Give a reason.

(iii) The following diagram shows a trade method of neatening this seam. Give precise instructions for working a similar method yourself. Name a suitable fabric on which the method could be worked. Give details of the type of thread, size of machine needle and the length and width of stitch you would recommend for use on the fabric.

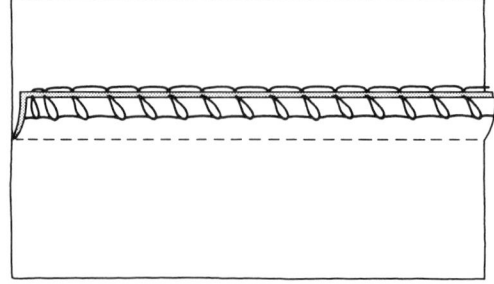

Question 10

In each of the following match one of Group A with one of Group B.

	Group A	Group B
a.	(i) Donkey	1. White
	(ii) Turkey	2. Blue
	(iii) Navy	3. Red
	(iv) Emerald	4. Brown
	(v) Winter	5. Green
b.	(i) Gored	1. Collar
	(ii) Turnback	2. Skirt
	(iii) Tie	3. Cuff
	(iv) Peter Pan	4. Yoke
	(v) Double	5. Neckline
c.	(i) French	1. Buttonhole
	(ii) False	2. Seam
	(iii) Shell	3. Hem
	(iv) Flannel	4. Dart
	(v) Bound	5. Edge
d.	(i) Paris	1. Lace
	(ii) Ric-rac	2. Cord
	(iii) Insertion	3. Elastic
	(iv) Shirring	4. Braid
	(v) Piping	5. Binding
e.	(i) Pure Silk	1. Yarn
	(ii) Tacking	2. Twist
	(iii) Stranded	3. Wool
	(iv) Tapestry	4. Cotton
	(v) Weaving	5. Thread
f.	(i) Presser	1. Lever
	(ii) Throat	2. Wheel
	(iii) Take-up	3. Clamp
	(iv) Balance	4. Plate
	(v) Needle	5. Foot
g.	(i) Cotton	1. Seersucker
	(ii) Nylon	2. Jersey
	(iii) Wool	3. Needlecord
	(iv) Neospun	4. Satin
	(v) Rayon	5. Gaberdine

	Group A	Group B
h.	(i) Dress	1. Measure
	(ii) Hem	2. Chalk
	(iii) Tailor's	3. Stand
	(iv) Tape	4. Mitt
	(v) Pressing	5. Marker
i.	(i) Straight	1. Mark
	(ii) True	2. Grain
	(iii) Weft	3. Line
	(iv) Fitting	4. Cross
	(v) Balance	5. Thread
j.	(i) Hem	1. Hole
	(ii) Slip	2. Loop
	(iii) Bar	3. Hem
	(iv) Rouleau	4. Stitch
	(v) Eyelet	5. Tack

Question 11

a. Give six qualities you would look for when purchasing the fabric to make this summer nightdress for yourself.

b. Name and describe the appearance of two suitable fabrics.

c. The underarm sections are faced with crossway strips. Why are crossway strips used?

d. (i) Explain the two diagrams below as indicated by the arrows numbered 1–11 to show that you understand the facing of the underarm section.
(ii) Name the stitch used in position 12. Why is a different stitch used here?
(iii) How would you ensure that the facings did not show on the R.S.?

e. (i) Name the type of seam illustrated in diagram B.
(ii) Why is this a useful seam for nightwear?
(iii) Put the following list in the correct order for working this type of seam:
R.S. together, tack, machine on fitting line, W.S. together, trim to 3 mm, tack, tacks out, machine 9 mm from edge, tacks out, match notches, raw edges together.
(iv) At which stages during the making of the seam should it be pressed?
(v) Name the particular points which should be watched when pressing the seam.
(vi) To which part of the garment should the seam finally be pressed?

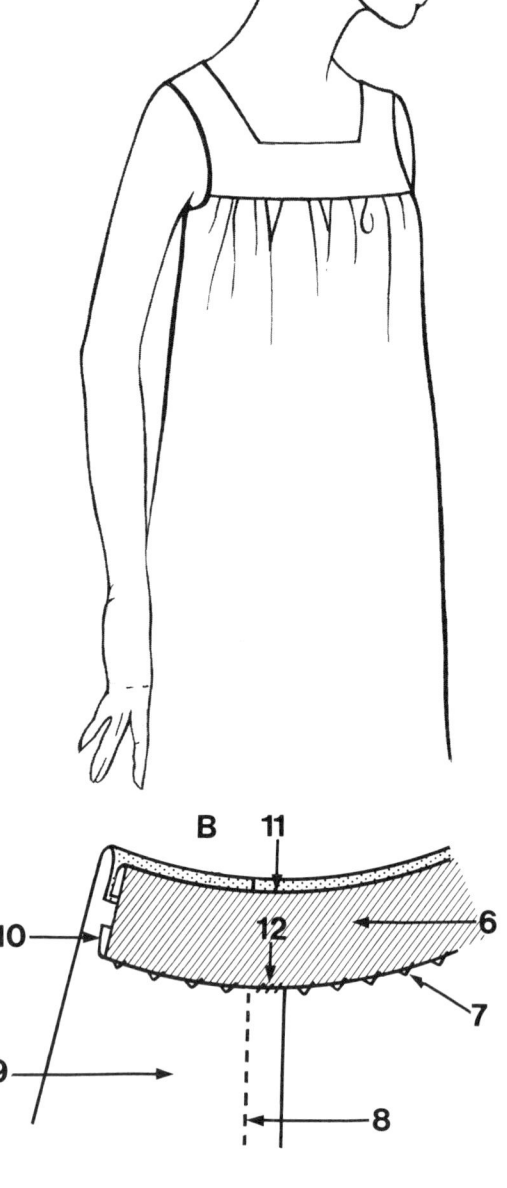

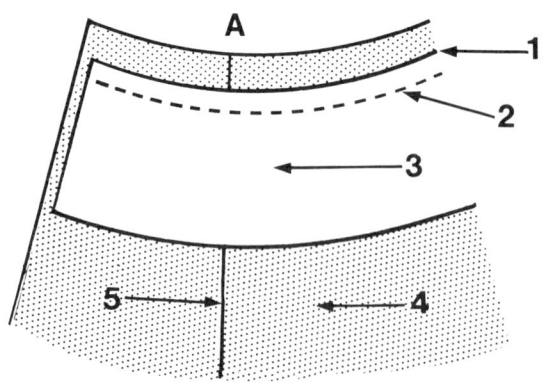

Question 12

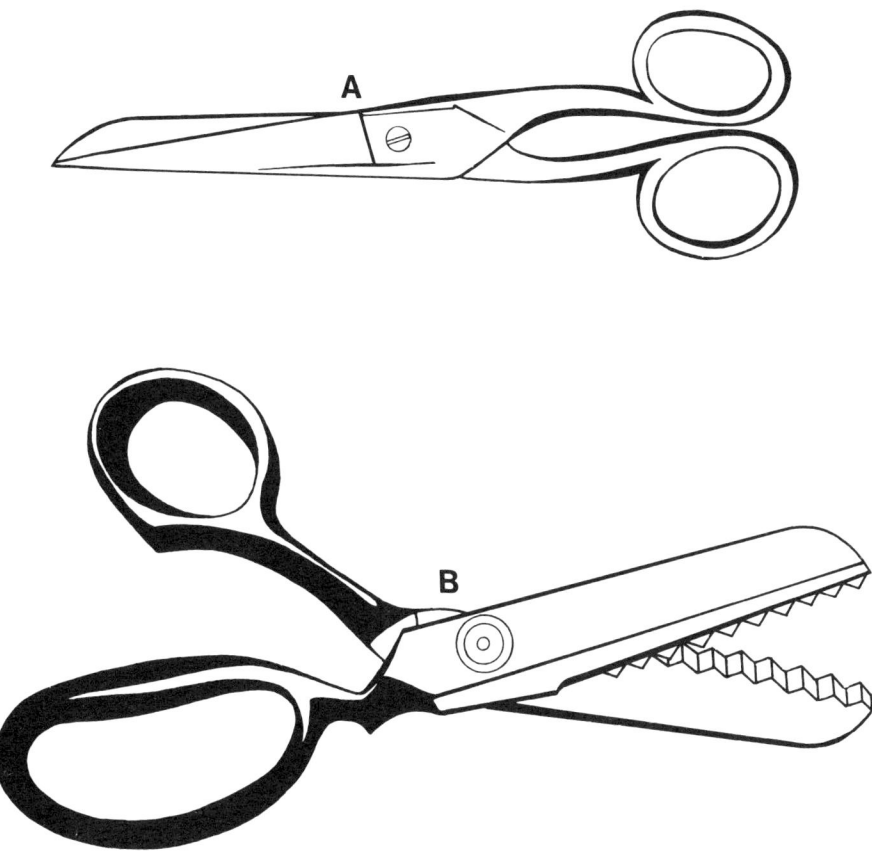

a. Name the two types of scissors illustrated and give two uses for each.

b. Describe and explain the function of the following machine parts:
   (i) Stop motion screw, (ii) Feed, (iii) Cover plate, (iv) Presser foot, (v) Take-up lever, (vi) Throat plate.

c. Give six points to be observed when winding a bobbin and inserting it into a sewing machine.

d. Giving details, explain the colour coding of machine needles.

e. Darning and beading needles both have specific uses. Explain the differences between these needles.

f. These needles are all size 8. Name them.

A

B

C

Question 13

a. Buttons are often used on garments, sometimes as decoration but normally as part of a fastening. Name five different ways of fastening with buttons. State a different position on a garment for each example.

b. Why is an opening usually required on a sleeve with a cuff which fastens?

c. (i) Explain the numbered arrows on the diagrams below to show that you understand the working of this opening. Name the opening.

(ii) Draw and label sketches to show how the section marked I has been worked. Name the process.

(iii) How wide would the section marked II be?

(iv) Give two methods of strengthening the opening at III and sketch them.

d. (i) Name two other types of opening which could be used in place of the one shown above.

(ii) Which of these three openings would be most suitable for a transparent fabric? Give a reason for your answer.

e. For the three openings referred to above, give the grain and size of the pieces which would be required for an 8-cm opening.

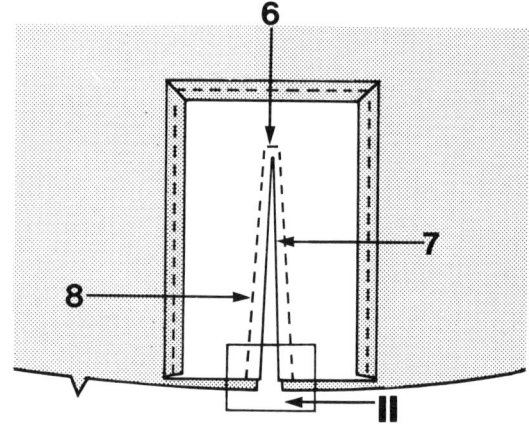

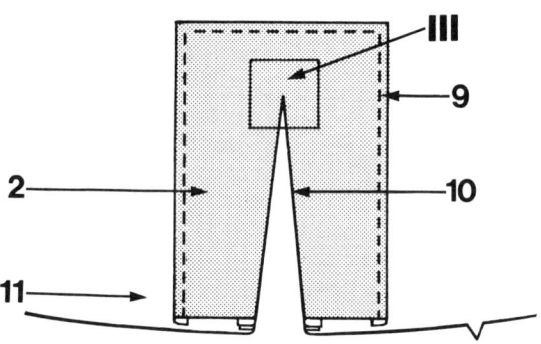

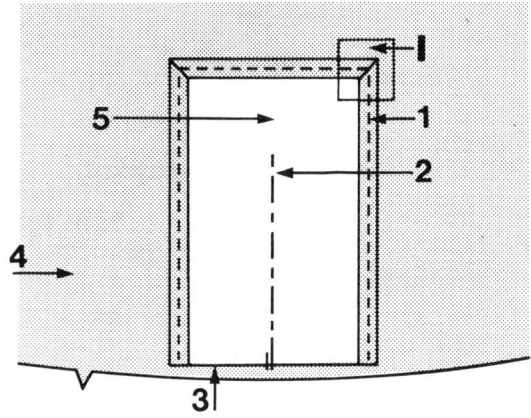

Question 14

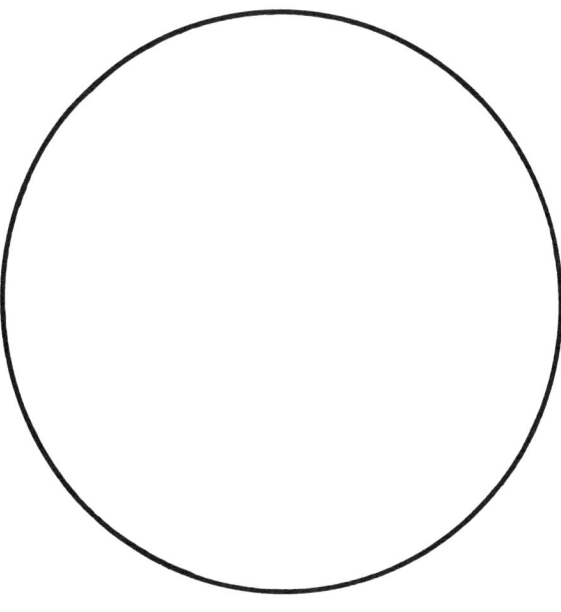
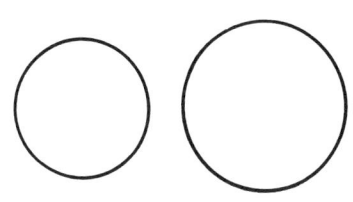

a.   Trace the largest circle shown above and in it use either or both of the small circles to create a suitable design for the top of a felt pincushion.

b.   (i) Suggest the type of thread and three decorative stitches to be used for the design. Indicate your colour scheme.
(ii) Make working diagrams of the three stitches to be used.

c.   (i) The pincushion will have a gusset 2 cm wide. How will you calculate the length of felt required to make the gusset?
(ii) Name a suitable stitch for joining the sections together.

d.   (i) Give your choice of filling for the pincushion and state two reasons for your choice.
(ii) Why is it desirable to use a pincushion?

e.   (i) How could you make a matching needlebook?
(ii) Suggest a suitable type of fabric for the leaves and a method for neatening the edges of them.
(iii) Show by a clearly-labelled diagram how you would fix the leaves into the needlebook.

f.   State three different types of needle you would put in the book. In each case give the particular purpose of the needle and the sizes which would be most useful.

Question 15

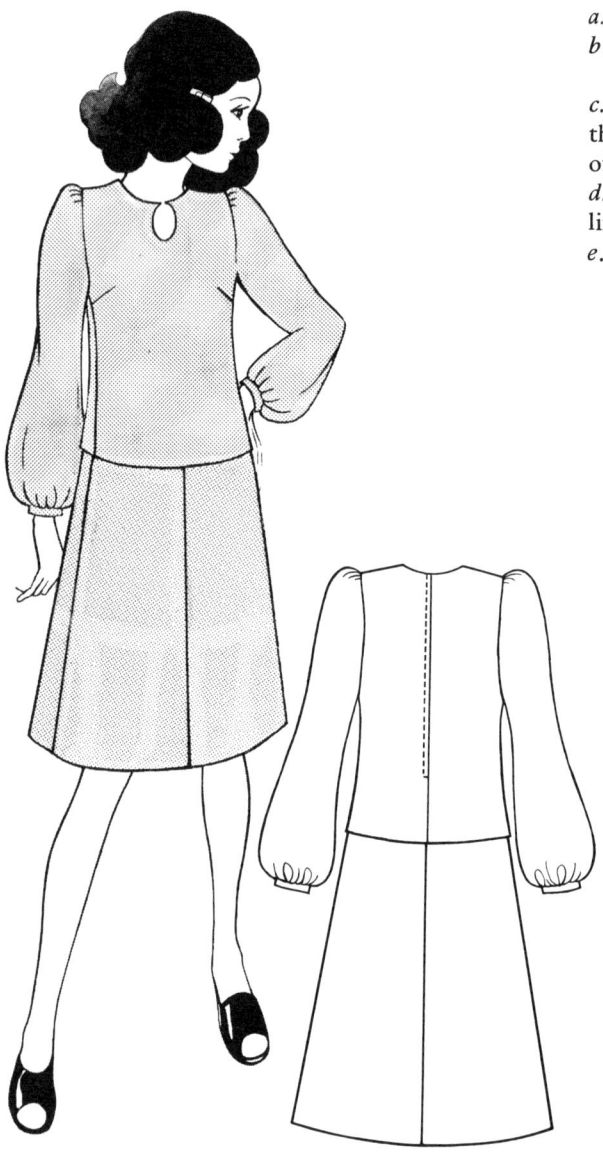

a. Describe the features of this blouse and skirt.

b. Name and describe a suitable type of fabric for:
   (i) the blouse, (ii) the skirt.

c. Give three reasons for your choice of fabric for the blouse and three different reasons for your choice of fabric for the skirt.

d. Name three suitable fastenings for the front neckline of the blouse.

e. (i) Copy diagram A opposite which represents 90 cm wide fabric. Trace and cut out the pattern pieces for the blouse which are shown in diagram B. With the aid of these pieces, plan an economical layout for the blouse, indicating the position for cutting the crossway strips required to finish the wrist edges. Label each piece.
   (ii) On your layout, insert the pattern markings you would find on each piece of the pattern.
   (iii) Estimate how much fabric would be required for making the blouse.

A

B

Fold

Selvedges

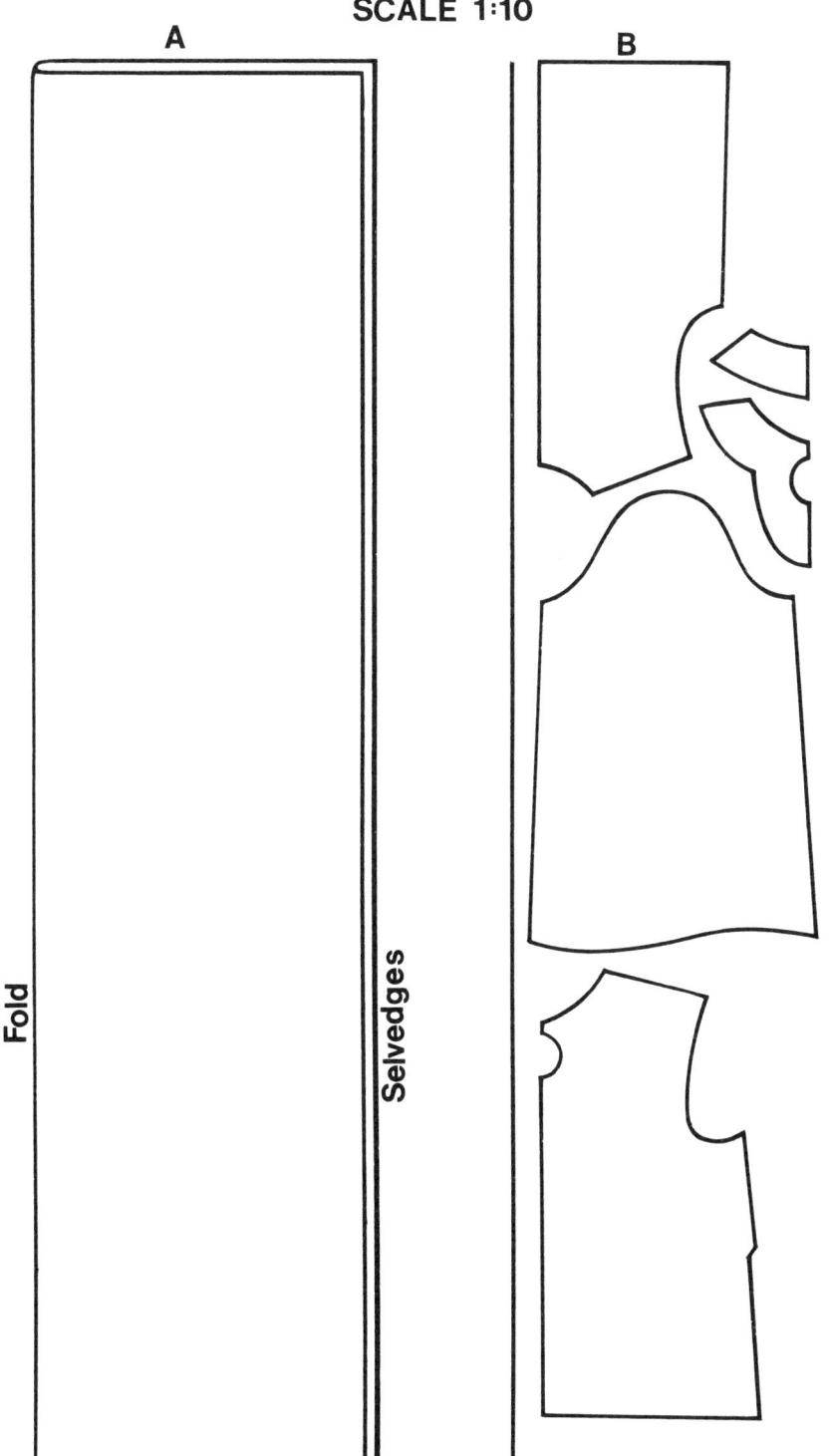

Question 16

Refer to the sketch of the blouse in Question 15.

a. (i) Explain the arrows as numbered in the diagram below to show your understanding of the neckline facing process.

(ii) Describe how you would anchor the facing to the shoulder seams when the facing has been turned to the W.S.

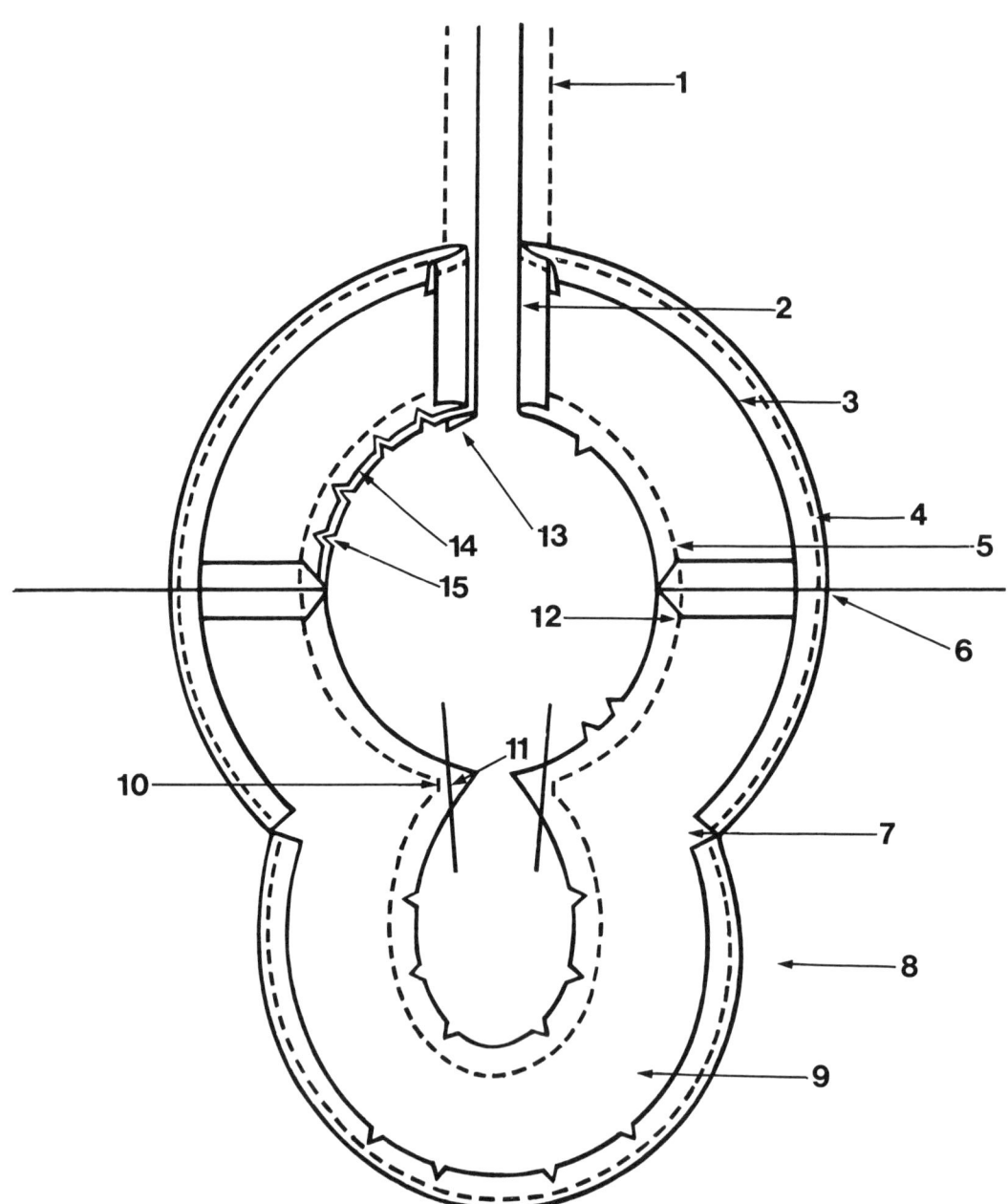

b. (i) Name the finish for the wrist edge shown in the diagram below.

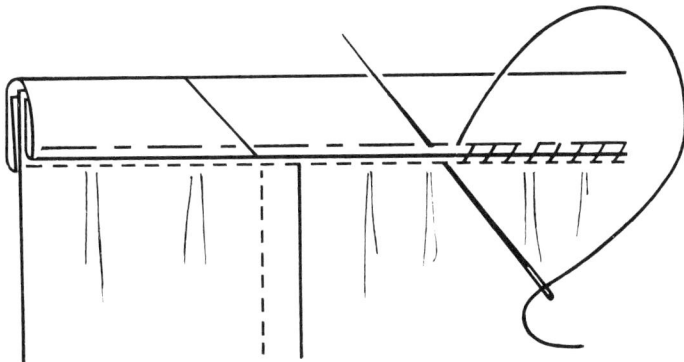

(ii) Using the diagram as a guide, list in correct order the fourteen stages for working this process.

c. Give five points which are matched when setting the sleeve into the armhole.

d. Suggest two ways of neatening the armhole after the sleeve has been inserted.

e. Name the undergarments you would wear with this blouse and skirt. Describe the qualities you would look for when purchasing these undergarments.

Question 17

a. (i) Name four styles (not makes) of zip fastener.
(ii) What four points should be considered when buying a zip fastener?

b. The diagrams show the preparation and the insertion of a zip fastener.
(i) Explain the numbered arrows to show your understanding of this process.
(ii) Draw a diagram showing the right side appearance of the finished process.
(iii) Give the name of this method of inserting a zip fastener.
(iv) State the names of two other methods of zip insertion.
(v) What should you consider when selecting which method to use? Give five points.

c. (i) Give two instances when it might be advisable to insert a zip fastener by hand.
(ii) Name the stitch you would use. Is this worked on the right or wrong side? What size and how close together should the stitches be?

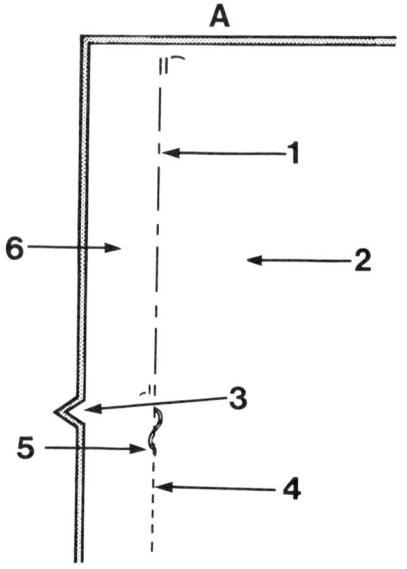

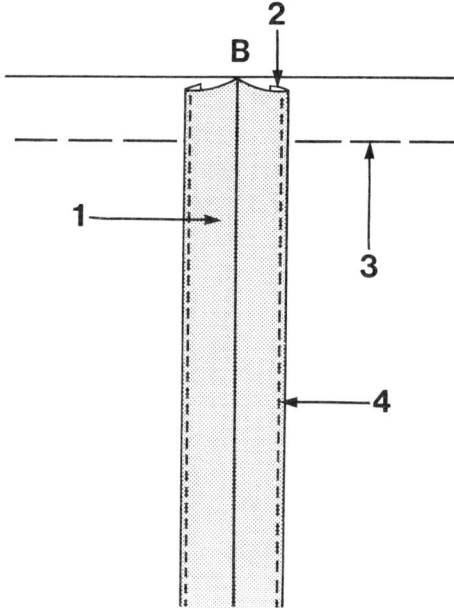

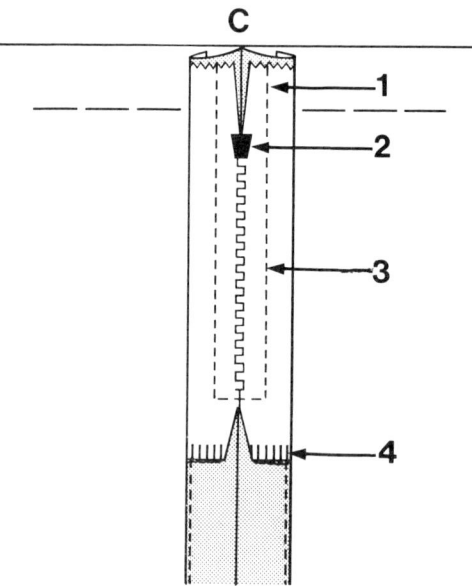

Question 18

Study the outfit illustrated below.

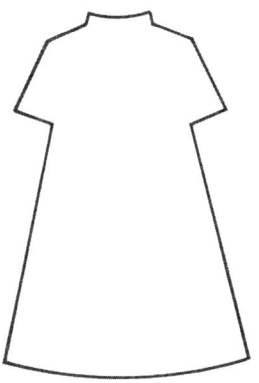

back view

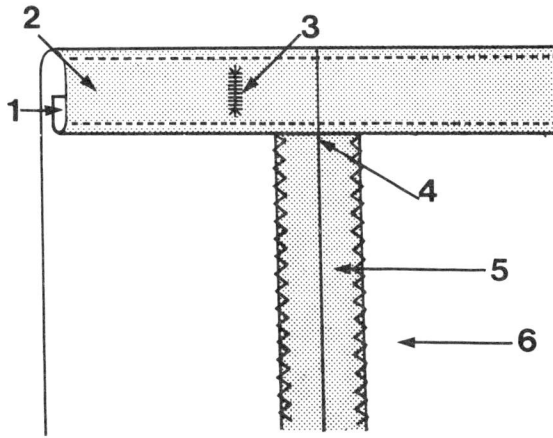

c. Name the seven pattern pieces required to make this outfit. Underline the one which would be placed to the fold in the layout and tick the one which could be cut on the cross.

d. Suggest two other forms of decoration which could be used to emphasise the front panel of the tunic.

e. The diagram below represents a section of the trouser waist casing. Explain the diagram as indicated by the numbered arrows to show that you understand the process.

a. Trace the outline of the back view of the tunic given above. Draw in and label the style details.

b. (i) Suggest and describe the appearance of a suitable fabric for this outfit.
(ii) List the notions required to make the outfit. For each notion state the quantity, type and size required.

f. (i) Suggest a suitable depth for the casing.
(ii) Give three reasons why there are two rows of machining on the casing.
(iii) Name the seam finish illustrated and state its width when completed.

21

Question 19

GENERAL INSTRUCTIONS

1. PRESS all seams open unless otherwise indicated Clip where necessary so seams will lie flat.

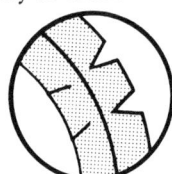

2. CLEAN-FINISH raw edges of seams, facings and hems by stitching 6 mm from edge and pinking.

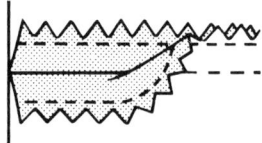

3. TRIM interfacing close to stitching after seams are stitched.

4. UNDERSTITCH to prevent facings from rolling out. To understitch, open out facing; stitch to seam allowance close to seam.

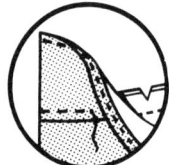

5. GATHERING is done along lines indicated on pattern, using long machine stitches.
6. TOP STITCHING — Thread machine with buttonhole twist *or* use regular thread.
7. KNIT FABRICS — Use polyester thread for all stitching.

a. The general instructions above are often given with paper patterns. Study them carefully and answer the following questions on each section.

1. Give four examples where this would be necessary.
2. (i) Name two fabrics for which the 'clean-finish' method would be suitable.
   (ii) State two other seam finishes which are more often used and name a suitable fabric for each method.
3. (i) Give two reasons for trimming the interfacing.
   (ii) Describe fully another method of applying non-fusible interfacing.
4. (i) State two positions where this process could be used.
   (ii) Besides understitching, an extra precaution is usually taken to prevent facings rolling out. State how this is done.
   (iii) What must be done to the seam allowances before understitching can take place? Give reasons for your answer.
5. (i) What other adjustment is usually made to the sewing machine besides lengthening the stitch?
   (ii) How many rows of machining are necessary for gathers? Where are they worked in relation to the F.L.?
   (iii) If the machining is worked on the R.S. of the garment, on which side are the threads which have to be pulled up?
6. (i) Explain the term 'top stitching'.
   (ii) Describe buttonhole twist.
   (iii) Why is buttonhole twist recommended?
   (iv) Name another thread specially made for top stitching and state its extra advantage.
7. (i) Name two polyester threads.
   (ii) Why must it be used for knitted fabrics?
   (iii) Name three knitted fabrics.

b. These four boxes are the fabric illustration key. Name each one.

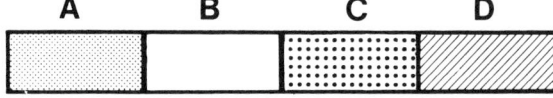

Question 20

a. Give ten general rules for darning.

b. 'Swiss darning' is worked contrary to some of the general rules. Study the diagram and explain clearly how Swiss darning is worked.

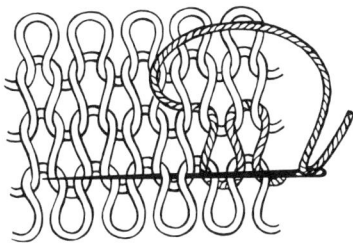

c. Name five other types of darn and state their specific purposes.

d. Study the diagrams below. Name the stitch illustrated. State when and why it is used and give instructions for working it.

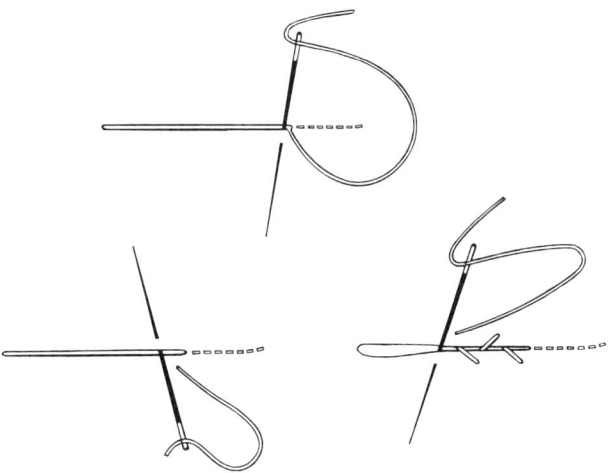

e. (i) Draw the shape of a tear which could be caused by catching a skirt on barbed wire.

(ii) On the diagram which you have drawn show the area which would need to be darned to make a satisfactory repair.

Question 21

a. Study the illustrations of printed fabrics below. Describe the type of design and for each state the type of layout which should be followed.

A

B

C

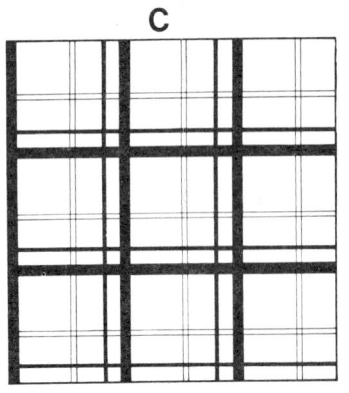

b. Make cardboard bodice shapes as given on page 74. Draw three rectangles and in them show how you would place these bodice pieces on each type of fabric (A, B and C) to give a correct and economic lay.

c. (i) Explain how the front bodice would be adjusted to give a C.F. seam and bias cut.
(ii) Show how this should be laid on fabric C when cutting on the bias to give a vandyke effect at the centre front.

d. Study the following diagram showing how to ensure that the checks match when the centre front seam is joined.

(i) Name the method used and explain the arrows as numbered.
(ii) Sometimes, even when this method is followed, the fabric tends to 'creep' when machining. Suggest two ways of eliminating this fault.

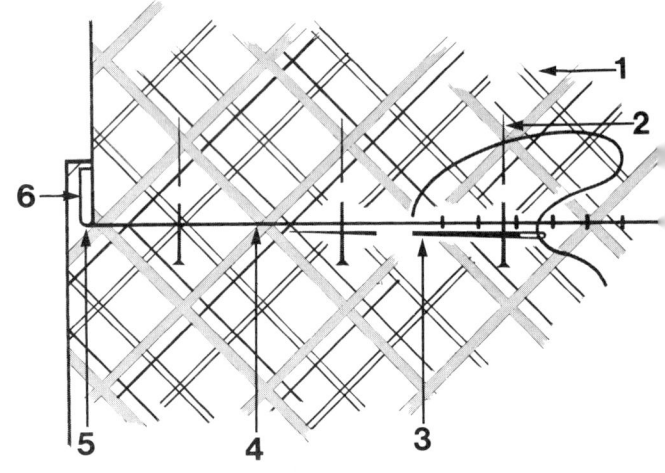

e. (i) Study the child's dress illustrated and name the pattern pieces which would be cut on the cross.

(ii) How would you ensure that these pieces did not stretch out of shape during the construction of the dress? Give a different method for each piece.

(iii) Name three positions on the dress where crossways strips would be used in different ways. Name the method of using the crossway and in each case state a suitable width of strip.

Question 22

a. Using the silhouettes inside front cover, draw the front and back views of a dress with the following features:
empire line bodice with gathers under the bust line; scoop neckline; fitted midriff section at the front and back; bishop sleeves with narrow cuffs fastening with one button and buttonhole; centre back zip; bias cut skirt; shoulder darts in back bodice; darts in back bodice to fit the midriff section.

b. Name and describe a suitable fabric for this dress and give three reasons for your choice.

c. List the notions which would be required to complete the dress. In each case give the quantity, type and size required.

d. (i) Which sections of the dress would be improved by interfacing?
(ii) Name a suitable type of interfacing and estimate the quantity required.

e. What type of buttonhole would you make on the cuff? Give two reasons for your choice. State the size of the buttonhole.

Question 23

If you were making the dress with the features described in Question 22:

a. Explain the special points which should be observed when:
(i) Working the gathers under the bustline,
(ii) Joining the midriff section to the bodice and skirt,
(iii) Inserting the zip fastener,
(iv) Facing the neckline,
(v) Setting in the sleeves,
(vi) Attaching the cuffs,
(vii) Preparing the hemline.

b. What equipment would be used for the final pressing of this dress? Give the order in which this work would be carried out.

c. Suggest three ways of giving this dress individuality. Use sketches to illustrate your ideas.

Question 24

a.   What should you do to your school blazer before taking it to the dry cleaners?

b.   List five general points which should be considered when removing stains from fabrics.

c.   The following substances are usually found in the home and can be used as stain removers:

milk, salt, methylated spirit, glycerine, lemon juice.
Name a stain which could be removed by each of these substances.

d.   Give brief details for the general care necessary for a pleated skirt made from woollen tweed.

e.   Write full notes on the care of tights or stockings.

f.   Clothes which are made carefully with well-chosen seams, etc. should wear well as extra strength may be given at weak points. Ready-made clothes are not always so well made. Suggest different ways in which the following could be strengthened:

(i) The base of an opening, (ii) A button sewn on to single fabric, (iii) The top of a pleat, (iv) Raw edges on the W.S., (v) Armhole seams.

g.   (i) Sketch three ways of strengthening the top of a patch pocket by machining.

(ii) If the pocket is to be hand stitched invisibly, how can this be strengthened on the W.S.?

h.   Study the diagram showing the strengthening at the underarm of a magyar sleeve and explain the arrows as numbered.

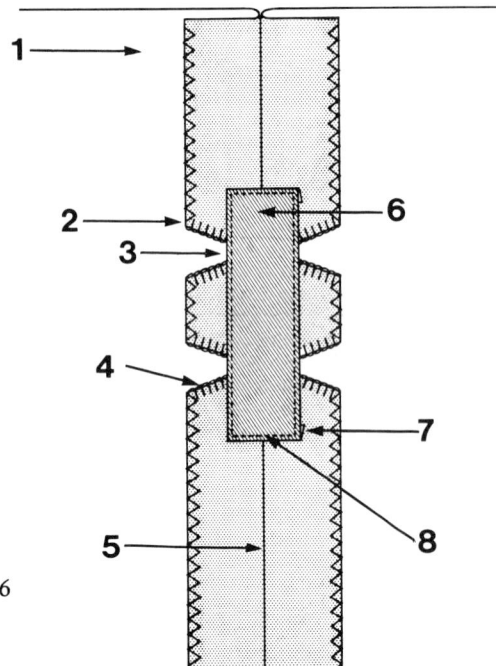

Question 25

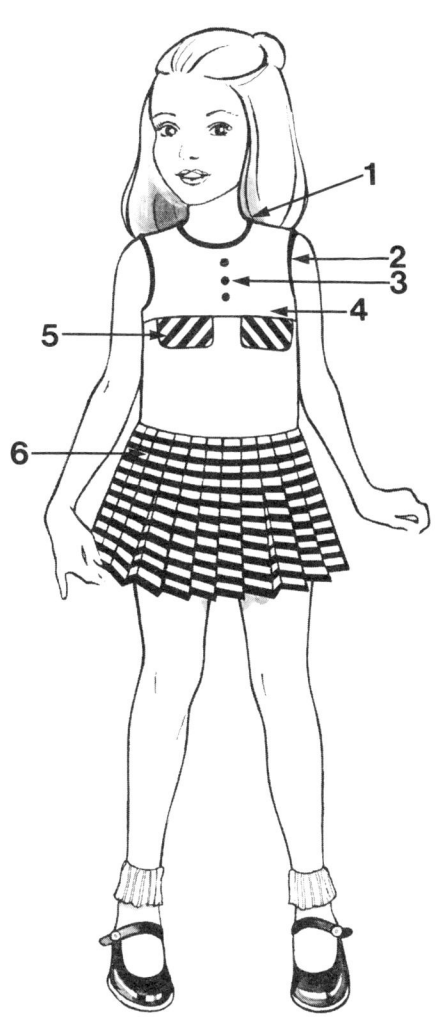

c. List the notions required to make the dress. In each case give the quantity, type and size or colour required.

d. The diagrams below show the making up of a flap for the dress.

    (i) What special care should be taken when cutting out the flaps?

    (ii) What do each of the arrows (1—7) indicate on the diagrams?

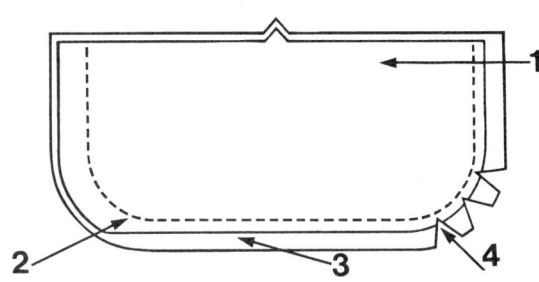

a. Name and describe the appearance of suitable mix and match fabrics for the child's dress illustrated above. Give five reasons for your choice.

b. Name the style features of the dress indicated by numbered arrows.

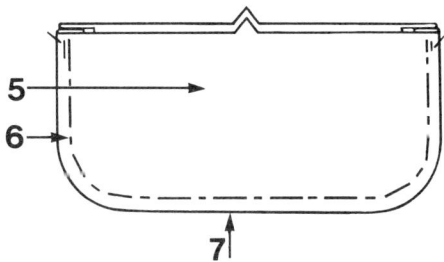

Question 26

a. This diagram shows the making of a cuff.
Name the processes indicated by the numbered arrows
and give different reasons why each is carried out.

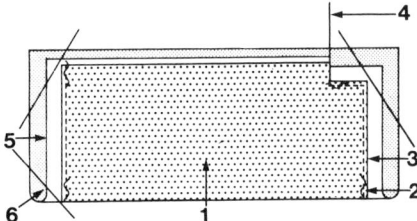

b. The following diagrams are taken from a pattern
primer (instruction sheet) and show an alternative
method of making a cuff. Amplify the instructions
which are in italics.

Baste INTERFACING 9 to
wrong side of CUFF 9. *Sew
invisibly* along foldline.

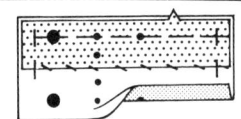

Turn in seam allowance on
long unnotched edge; press.

Pin sleeve to cuff between
seamline and large •, placing
small ••'s at underarm seam.
Pull threads to adjust fulness.
Baste. *Stitch. Trim.* Press seam
toward cuff.

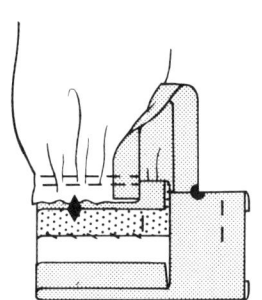

Turn cuff to outside along foldline. *Stitch ends. Trim.*

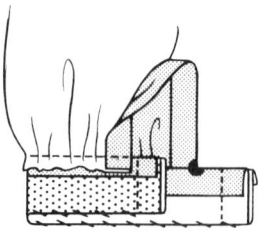

Turn cuff to inside. *Slipstitch
remaining edge over seam.*

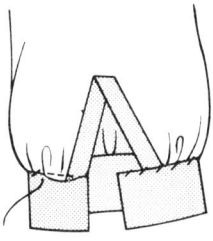

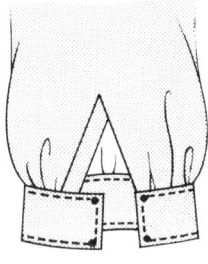

Top-stitch 5 mm from edges of
cuff, *pivoting* at small •'s, as
shown.

c. (i) Which method do you prefer and why?
(ii) Trace this sketch of the finished cuff and
mark clearly the positions for the button and
buttonhole fastening.

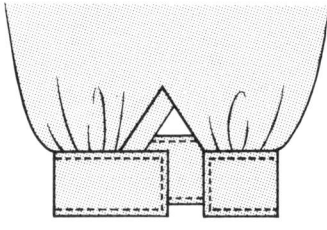

(iii) How would these positions be printed on the
paper pattern for the cuff?

Question 27

a. (i) With the aid of the diagram below explain how a zip tape can be made to lie along the fitting line.
(ii) Give two instances when it would be advisable to use this method.
(iii) What should be done to the section marked I and why?

c. Study the three diagrams C D and E, showing how to make a neat corner.
(i) Name the method.
(ii) Suggest where this method could be used.
(iii) Write notes for working the process as shown in the diagrams.
(iv) If this method were being used on the corners of an evenweave linen place mat, what else should be done at the final stage?

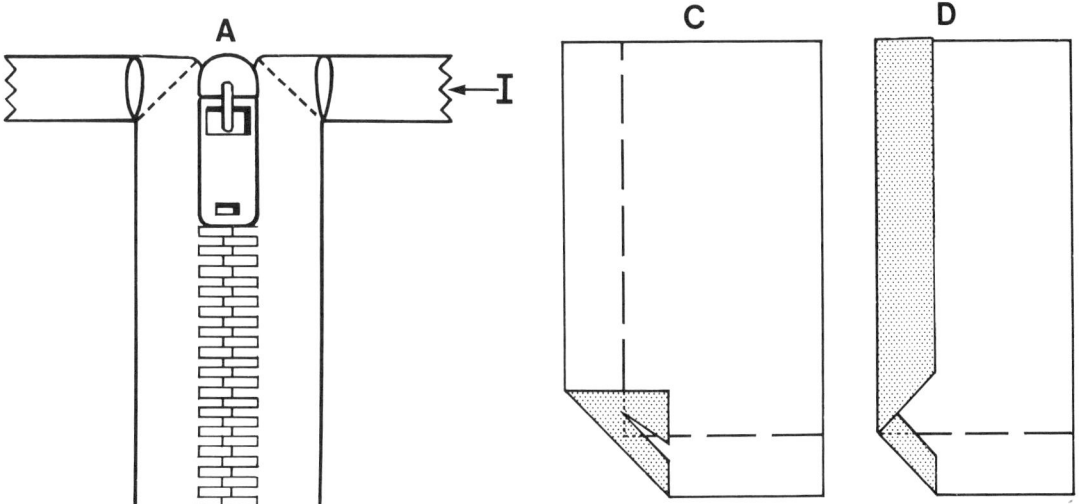

b. (i) What does diagram B show?
(ii) When and why is it useful?
(iii) Explain how to make and attach the loop as shown in the diagram.

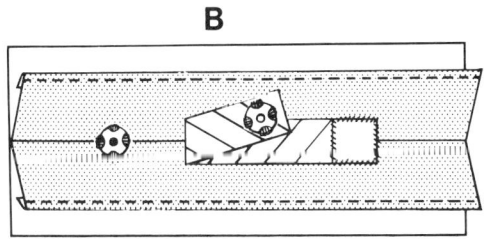

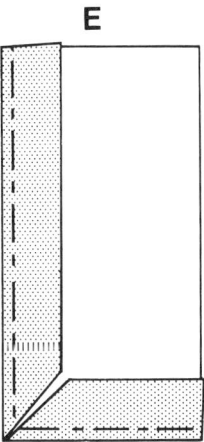

Question 28

a. When preparing and laying a dress pattern on the fabric before cutting out, give the correct order in which you would do the following:

pin, plan the layout, prepare the fabric, adjust the pattern, study the pattern and instructions, check the pattern measurements.

b. Trace the pattern for a front bodice shown below.

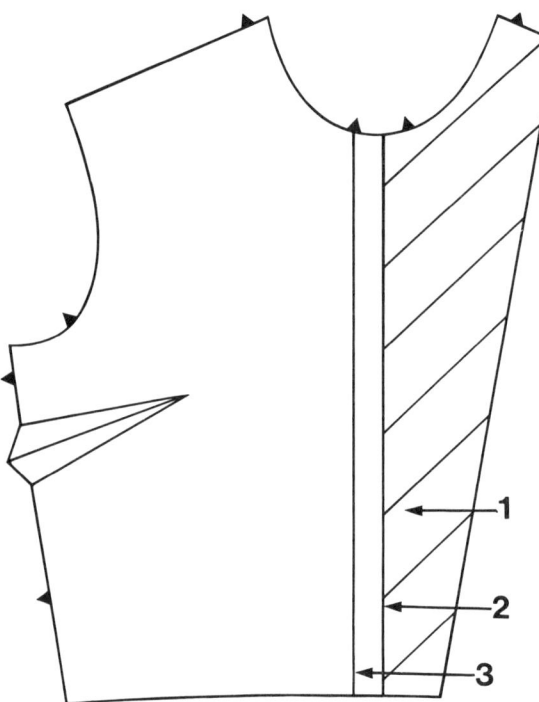

c. Explain the numbered arrows on the diagrams below to show that you understand the process of making and applying a patch pocket.

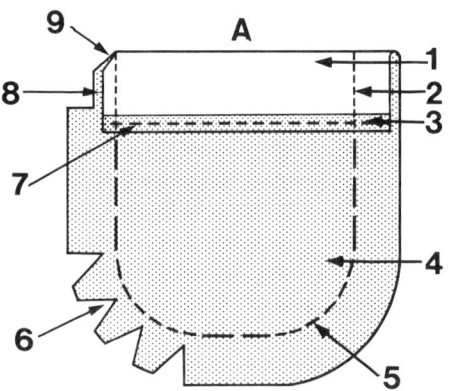

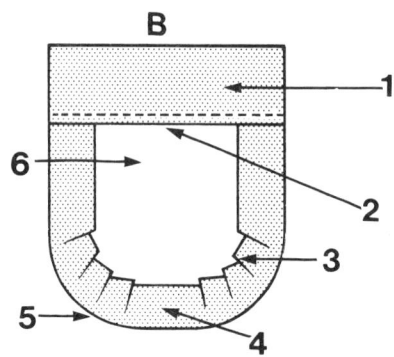

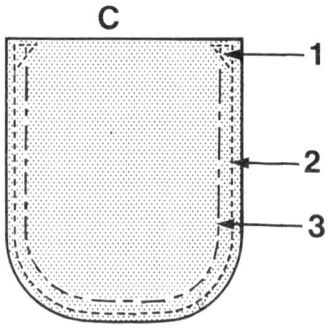

(i) Label the pattern section 1 and the pattern lines 2 and 3.

(ii) Mark the positions for four buttonholes.

(iii) The point of the bust dart is slightly too low. Redraw the dart in the correct position.

(iv) Mark in the fitting line and state the width of the seam allowance.

(v) Mark the lines where you should shorten the length and increase the width of the pattern.

(vi) On the diagram draw the pattern marking for a breast pocket.

(vii) Draw and name two other pattern markings which would be printed on this pattern piece.

Question 29

a. Name the style features as indicated by the numbered arrows. Use at least two words in each case.
b. Name the nine pattern pieces required to make the smock.
c. State three positions where interfacing should be used.
d. How could mix and match fabrics be used to add interest to this garment?

e. Study the following diagrams which would be given with the pattern and write instructions for working the process shown.

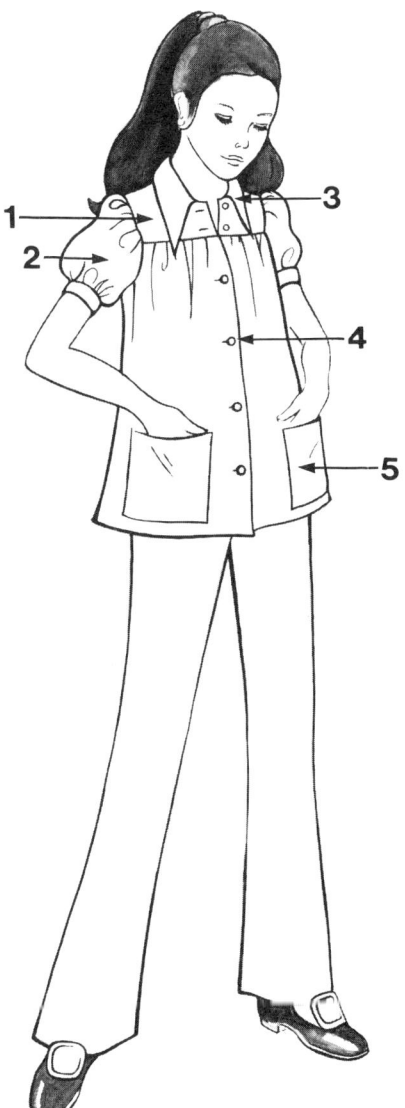

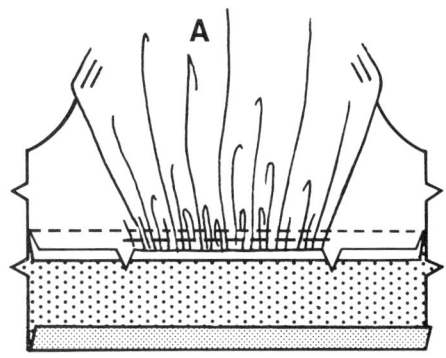

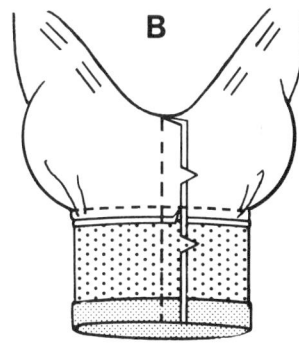

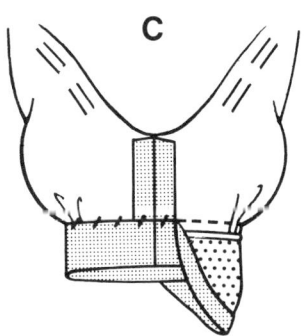

Question 30

a. (i) This is a care label for a blouse made of blue cotton/polyester lawn. Copy the label and complete the information which would be given to help you take care of the garment.

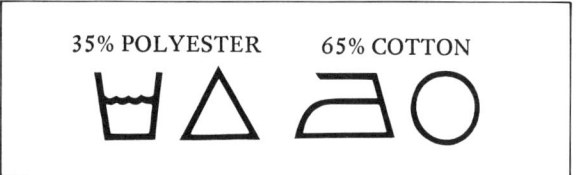

(ii) Explain fully each of the symbols.

b. Write as fully as possible about each of the following trade marks or symbols.

c. (i) Give the details which would be found on the care label of a jumper with a 'Superwash' finish.
(ii) How would you care for a garment made from white Celon?

1

TREVIRA®

2

ANTI STAT 3

WEAR DATED TRADE MARK

Monsanto

4

5

KORATRON®

6

Celon

7

Question 31

In the parts of this question where there are dashes, give words to complete the sentence.

a. Study this sketch of a dress which has a double yoke and describe the style details where indicated by numbered arrows, using at least two words in each case.

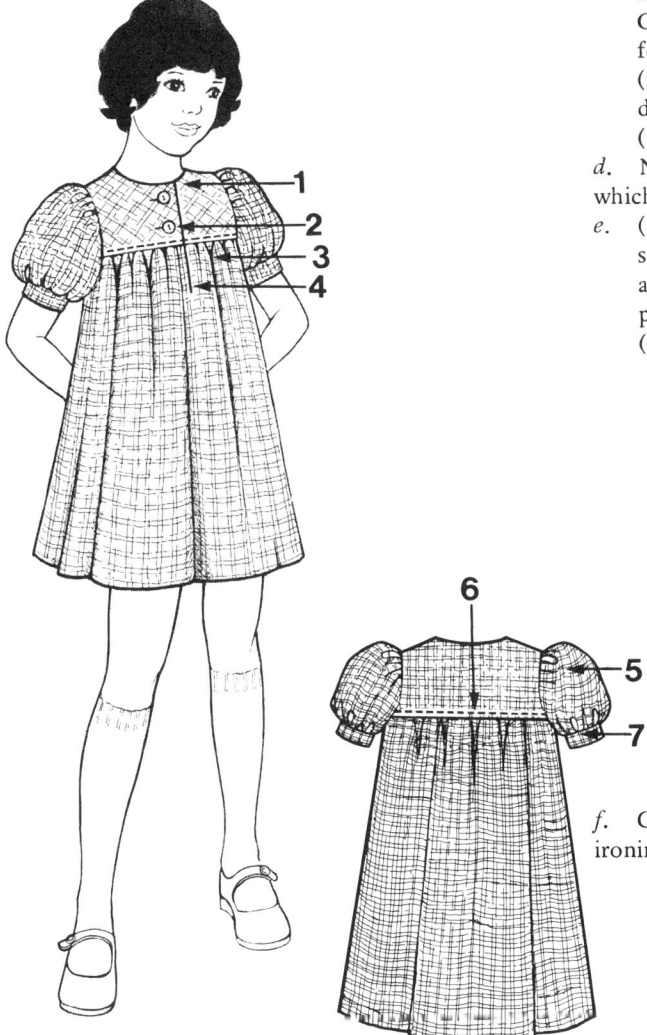

b. (i) Nylon seersucker would be a suitable fabric for making this dress.
Nylon is a ____ fibre and is made from ____ , ____ and ____ .
(ii) Give four reasons why this fabric is suitable for this dress.

c. (i) Cotton gingham would also be suitable for making this dress.
Cotton is a ____ fibre and is grown chiefly in the following three areas: ____ , ____ and ____ .
(ii) Cotton gingham is a fabric with a woven ____ design.
(iii) Name two other ways of colouring fabrics.

d. Name and describe two other types of fabric which would be suitable for this dress.

e. (i) This enlarged diagram of a piece of fabric shows a ____ weave. The ____ threads pass alternately under and over the ____ threads to produce this weave.
(ii) Name two other types of weave.

f. Give the order of work to be followed when ironing the cotton gingham dress after laundering.

Question 32

Refer to the sketch for Question 31.

a. (i) These are five of the pattern pieces for the dress.

Name each one.

(ii) Name the pattern piece which is missing.

b. Trace and cut out the pattern pieces for the dress from A and make your own piece for the one that is missing.

(i) Trace diagram B which represents 90 cm wide fabric, and use the pieces to plan an economical layout for the dress.

(ii) Draw round the pattern pieces and number each piece as indicated.

(iii) Explain how to estimate the quantity of fabric which would be required for the dress.

(iv) List three items it would be necessary to buy to complete the dress.

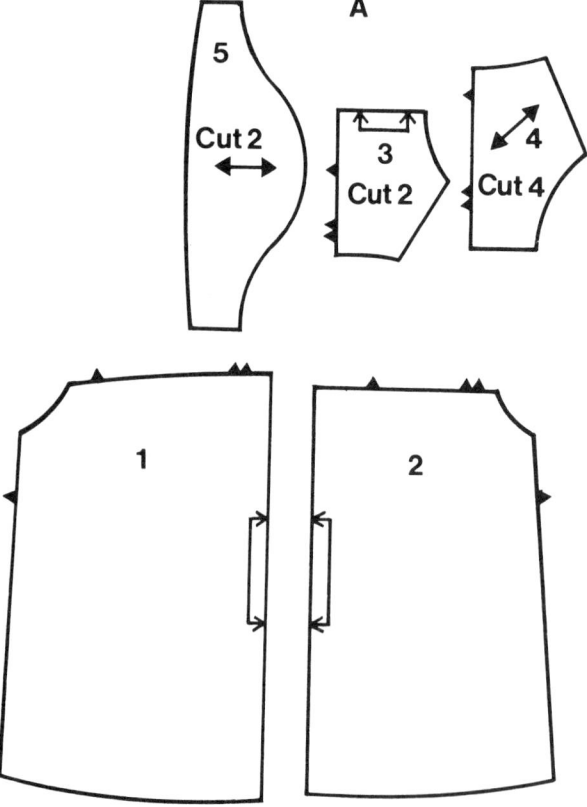

34

c. Study diagrams A and B for making up a double yoke. Explain the arrows as numbered.

d. The yoke of the dress would be joined to the skirt by an overlaid seam. Explain the diagram below as indicated by the numbered arrows.

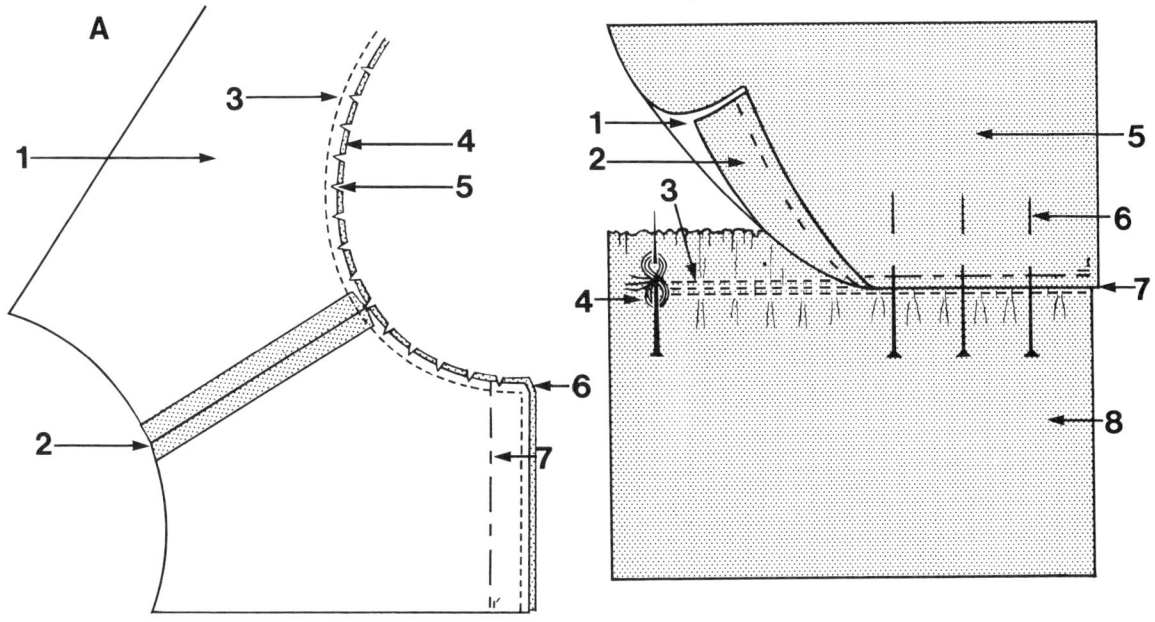

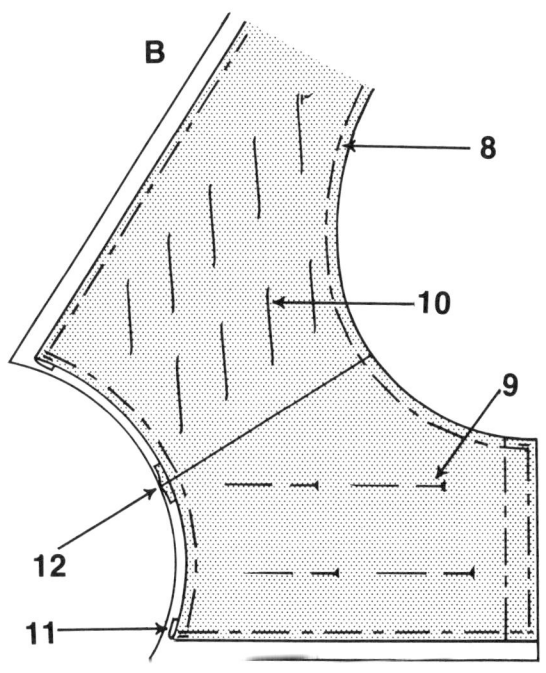

e. Name four different permanent stitches which could be sewn by hand when making this dress and say where each one would be used.

Question 33

a. (i) Describe the following threads:
1 Coton à broder, 2 Sylko perlé, 3 Soft embroidery, 4 Stranded thread, 5 Fresca, 6 Perlita, 7 Tapestry wool.
(ii) State a type of embroidery and one fabric for which each thread is suitable. Give different examples.
(iii) Give the correct type and size of needle for each thread.
b. Describe in detail how to set up an automatic machine for embroidery.

Question 34

Study diagrams A and B showing the treatment of a curved hem.

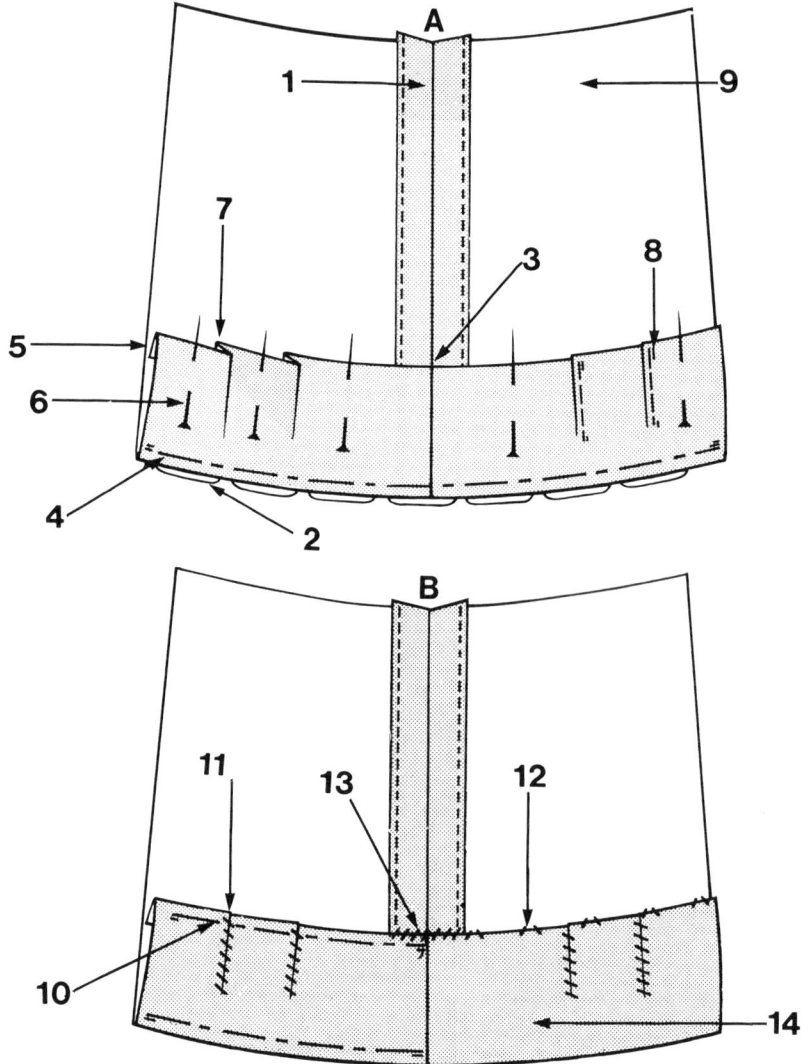

a. Explain the arrows as numbered on the diagrams to show that you understand fully the method and sequence for completing the process.

b. (i) Name two fabrics for which this method would be suitable and state a desirable depth of hem.

(ii) Choose one of the fabrics given in *b* (i) and state the type and size of thread and needle to be used.

(iii) Give full details for pressing the completed hemline.

c. Study diagrams C and D.

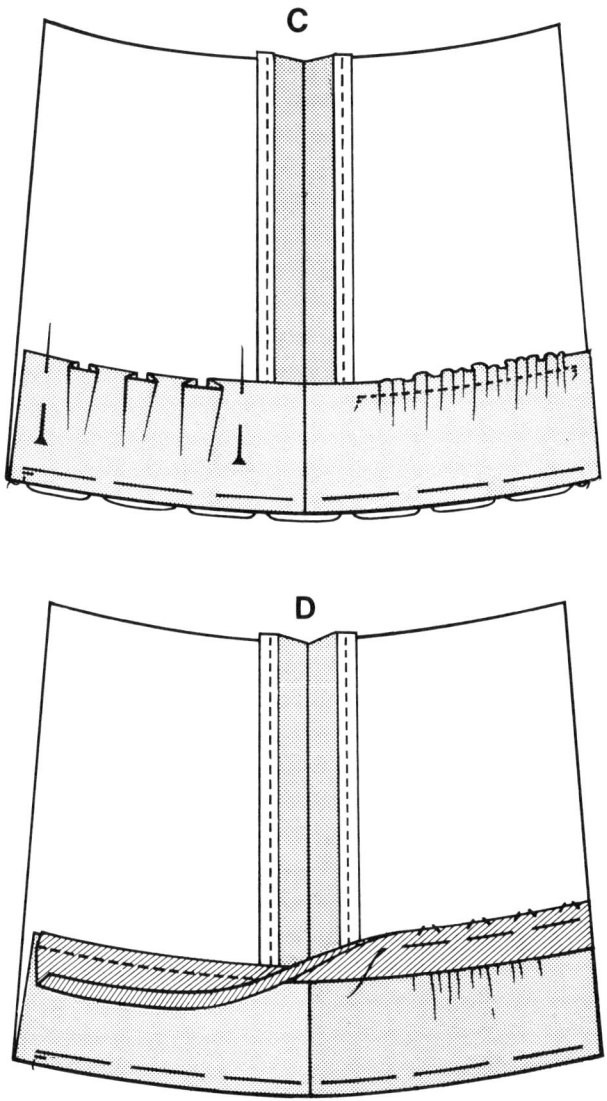

The hem is the same shape as in the previous diagrams,
but the treatment of the hem is different.
    (i) List these differences and give a reason for
    them.
    (ii) What differences would there be in the method
    of pressing the completed hemline?
d. When would the following be used to neaten a
hem?
    (i) Paris binding, (ii) A shaped facing.

Question 35

a. (i) Supply the missing words to complete the instructions for calculating the size of fabric required for making a stiffened belt:

Length on _____ grain = _____ measurement + 3 cm _____ + _____ cm overwrap + 5 cm _____ _____.

Width = _____ x finished _____ + _____ turnings of _____.

(ii) Name three types of stiffening suitable for belts.

(iii) Explain the numbered arrows (1–10) on the two-stage diagrams to show how the belt is made. Name the stitch which would be used in position 11.

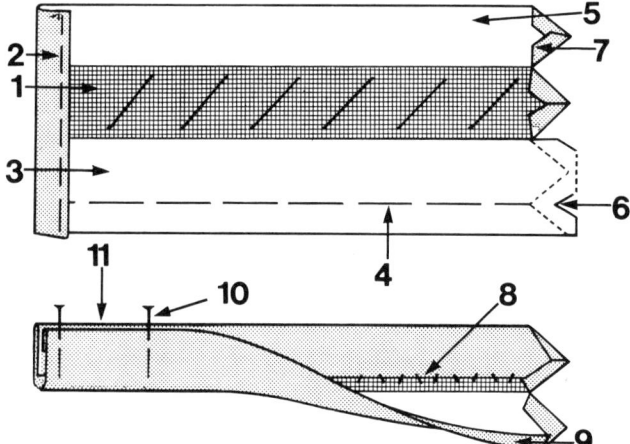

(iv) Study the diagram of the completed belt and explain the arrows as numbered.

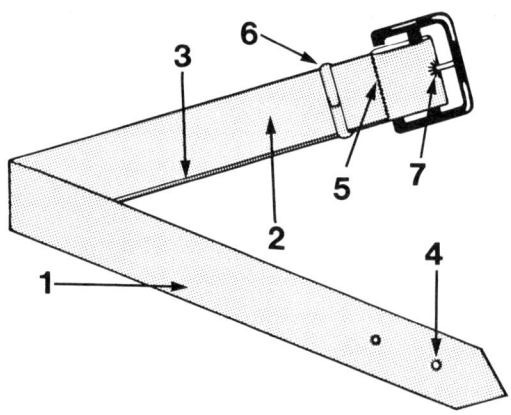

b. (i) Give stage by stage instructions for making an eyelet as illustrated in diagrams A, B and C.
(ii) Diagram D shows an alternative method of neatening the eyelet hole. What is the advantage and the disadvantage of this method?

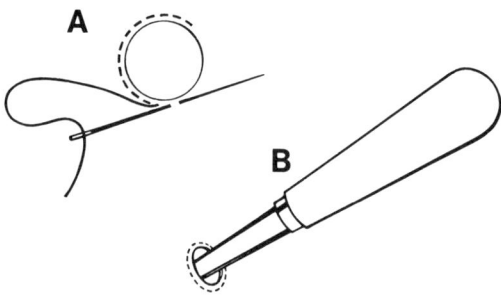

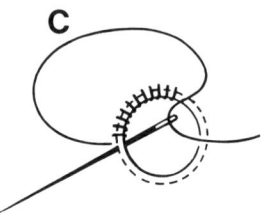

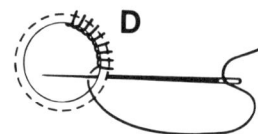

c. (i) Laced eyelet holes may be used to fasten garments. Name three types of laces which may be used.
(ii) State two positions where this method of fastening could be used.
(iii) What type of opening must be used?

Question 36

Question 37

a. Study the weave diagrams below. Dealing with each one separately:

(i) Name the weave illustrated, (ii) Explain its construction, (iii) Name a fabric so produced.

A

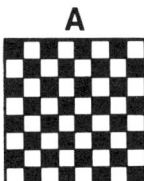

B

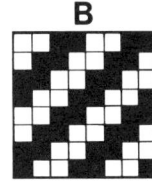

C

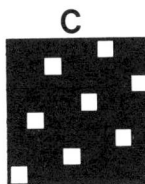

D

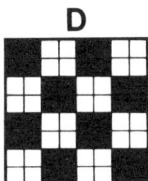

b. Explain the following terms:
(i) Straight grain, (ii) Selvedge, (iii) True cross, (iv) Bias.

Draw a diagram to illustrate your answer.

c. Name four pile fabrics.

Study the sketch of the blouse.

a. Name the type of sleeve.

b. Sketch the shape of the pattern piece for the front of the blouse. On this draw and label the following pattern markings:

place to fold, fitting line, notches, lengthening or shortening lines, position for control of fullness at neck, sleeve and waist.

c. Three different methods could be used for controlling the fullness at the neck, sleeve and waist to give the effect shown. Name these.

d. Name and describe a suitable type of fabric for the blouse and give four reasons for your choice.

e. Bearing in mind your answers to (*c*) and (*d*), list all the notions which would be required to complete the blouse. For each, state the quantity, type and size or colour required.

Question 38

a.   (i) State the most suitable length of zip fastener for
a side seam opening.
(ii) How is the zip fastener placed in relation to
the waist seam?

b.   Write stage by stage notes for each of the following diagrams which show the preparation of the garment and the insertion of a zip fastener into the side
seam of a dress.

A   **B**   **C**

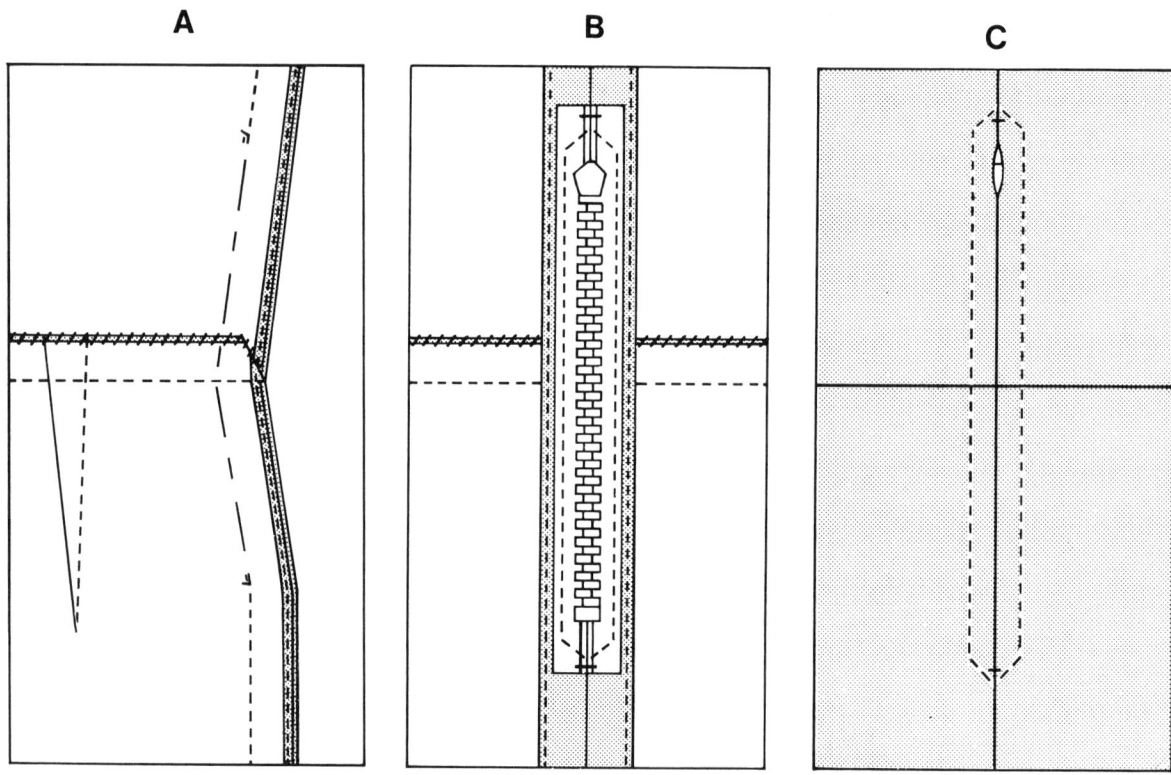

c. (i) Name the alternative opening for the side seam
of a dress which is shown in diagram D.

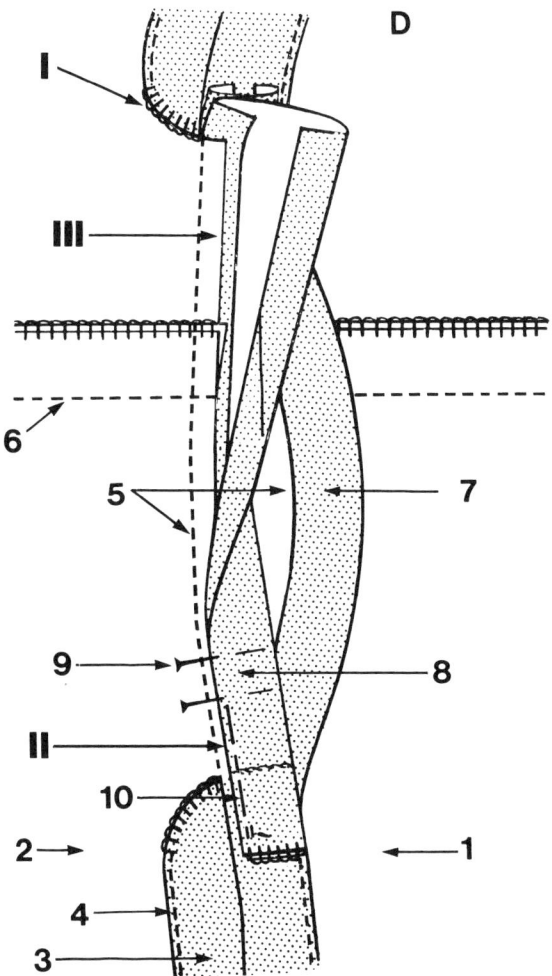

D

(ii) How will this opening be fastened?
(iii) Study the diagram and explain the arrows as
numbered to show that you understand how the
process is worked.
(iv) Why is the treatment marked I necessary?
(v) Name the stitch which will be used to secure
the fold at II.
(vi) Why is the seam allowance trimmed as shown
at III?
(vii) If this opening is used with a French seam,
how will the process differ from that shown in
diagram D?

41

Question 39

a. Name the types of collar illustrated below. Select the appropriate neckline shape for each one and suggest a different garment for which each collared neckline would be suitable. Tabulate your answer.

b. Which of the styles of collar shown below would be most becoming for a person with a short neck? Give reasons for your answer.

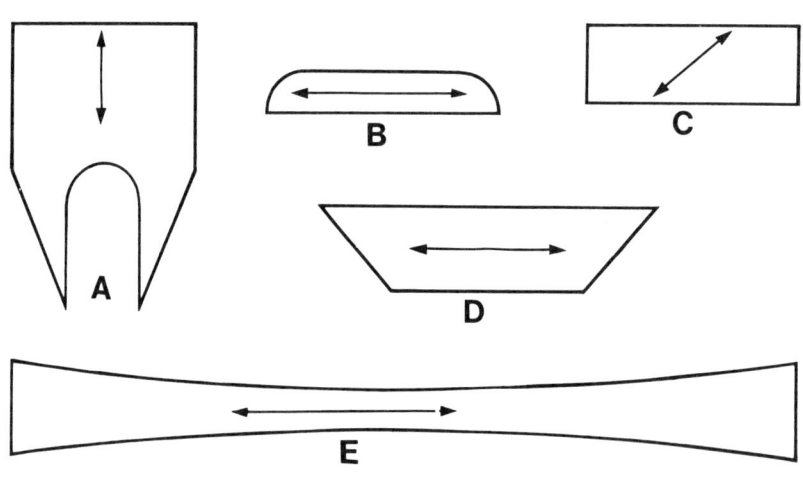

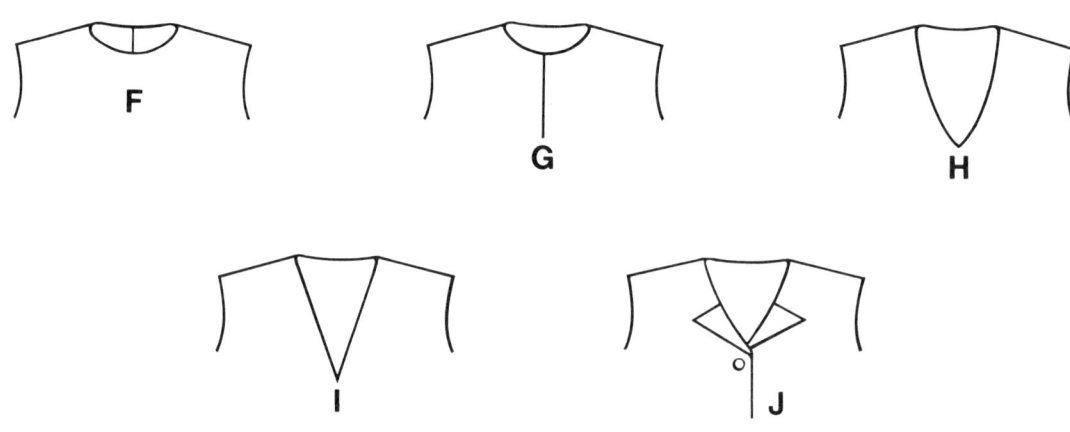

c. Trace the following outline of a collar pattern. On your tracing draw and label five markings you would expect to find on the pattern.

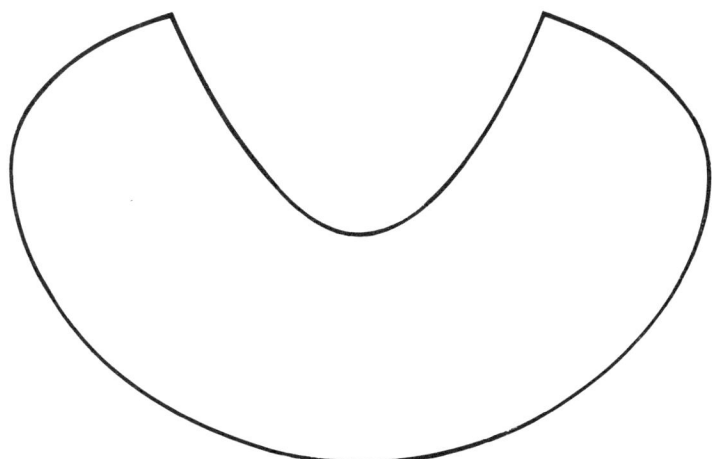

d. Study the diagram below showing the preparation of this collar and explain the numbered arrows.

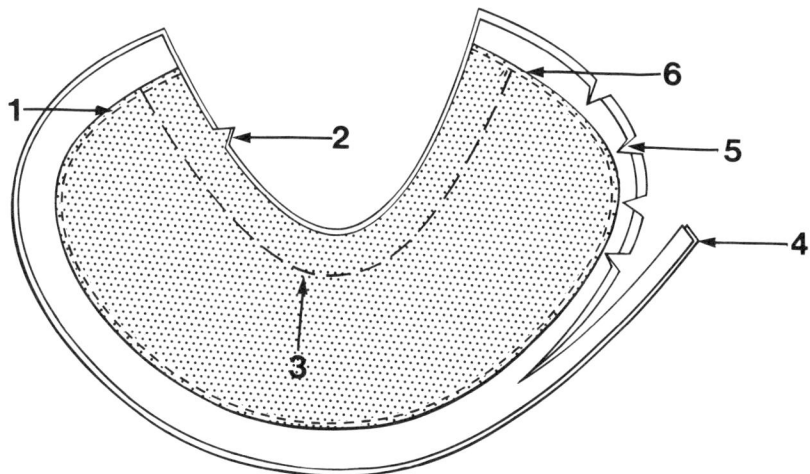

e. Give full details for completing the making up of this collar.

f. (i) Name three methods of attaching this collar to the neck of a child's dress which has a yoke.
(ii) Which is the most satisfactory method and why?

Question 40

a. (i) List the pattern pieces necessary to make this pinafore dress.
(ii) Underline those which should be placed to the fold in the layout.
(iii) On which section of the pinafore dress will the straight grain be horizontal when the dress is worn?

b. Tucks are used to decorate this garment. Draw a diagram to show how these would be indicated on the pattern piece.

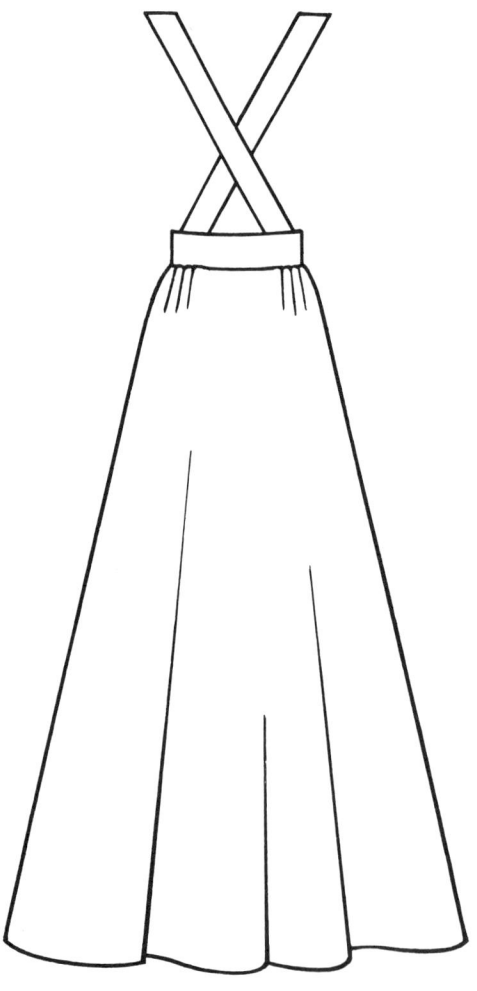

c. (i) Name the method for disposing of the fullness at the waist of the skirt.
(ii) How would this be shown on the pattern piece?
(iii) Name four other methods of disposing of fullness.

d. Study the following diagram showing how the bib is joined to the waistband and explain the arrows as numbered.

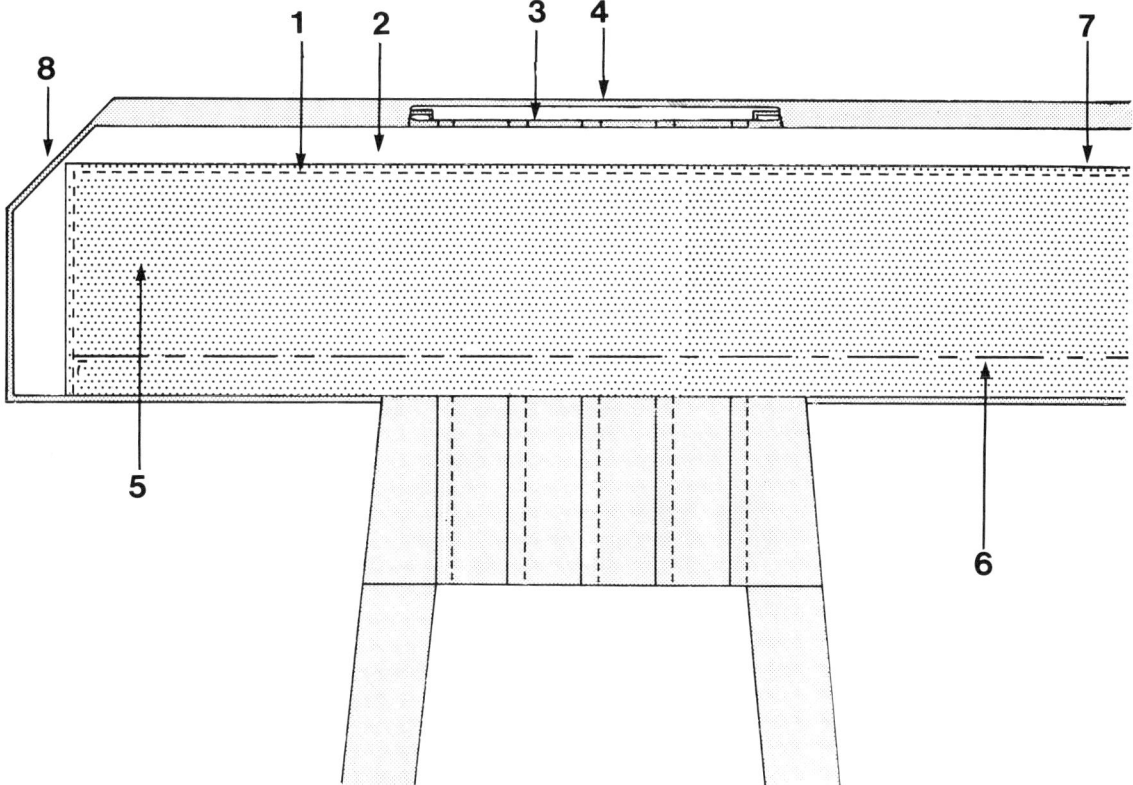

e. Explain fully the next stages in this process – before attaching to the skirt.

Question 41

a. (i) Name the styles of pleat shown in the following skirt illustrations.

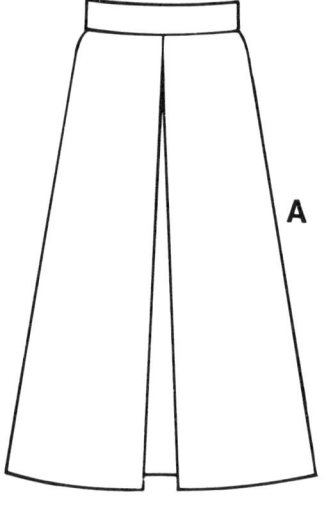

A

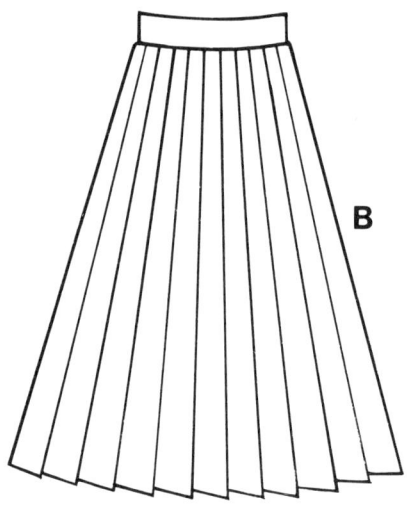

B

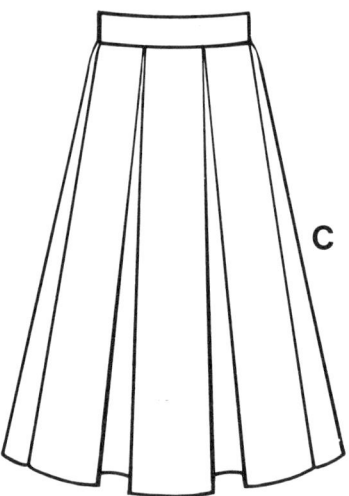

C

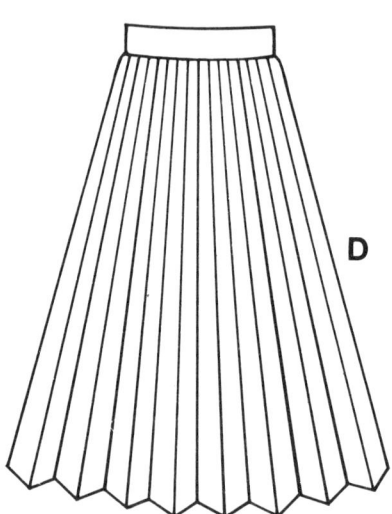

D

(ii) Which type of pleating is best carried out commercially?

b. (i) What points should you consider when selecting fabrics for pleated skirts?
(ii) Suggest a different type of fabric for each skirt shown in (a).

c. (i) How could the top of the pleat shown in illustration A be strengthened decoratively by hand?

(ii) Give a diagram to show how the strengthening is worked.

(iii) State the type of thread, and type and size of needle to be used.

d. For the skirt illustrated in B, describe in detail how you would use a sewing machine to keep the pleats in.

e. On skirt C you decide to stitch the pleats as far as the hipline. Show by diagrams two methods of doing this.

f. How would you store skirt D when not in use so that the pleats stay sharp?

g. It is possible that skirt A will have an inlay section for the pleat.

(i) Draw the shape of this pattern piece and mark and label the pattern markings you would find on it.

(ii) The following diagram shows a method of finishing the pleat at the hem. Explain this method and say why it is so satisfactory.

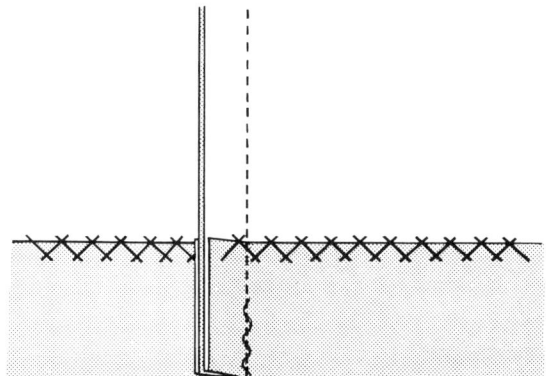

Question 42

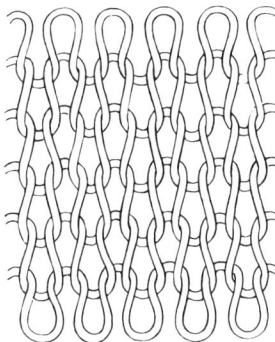

a. What method of fabric construction does this diagram show? Explain the diagram to show how the fabric is constructed.

b. Name five articles of clothing commonly made from this method of construction.

c. Name six types of yarn which are currently available for this method of fabric construction.

d. Name five different types of fabric made by this method.

e. Give five advantages of using fabrics made by this method for dressmaking.

f. Select one of the fabrics you have given for (*d*) and give details of the type of thread, machine needle and stitch size required to make a satisfactory garment. Give a reason for your answer in each case.

g. From the articles of clothing you have mentioned in (*b*), select two which are quite different from each other. Stating the yarn from which each is made, give full details for laundering them, including the care label which should be sewn into each one.

Question 43

c. The following terms are printed on the pattern envelope: 'Use unbonded knits' and 'Bias printed fabric'. Explain each of these terms and say why it is necessary to give this information on the envelope.

d. Name one natural and one man-made yarn knitted into fabrics. Underline the one you would choose for this outfit and give five reasons for your choice.

e. (i) The shoulder seams of the pinafore dress would be stabilized. Study the diagram below and explain the numbered arrows to show that you understand how this is done.

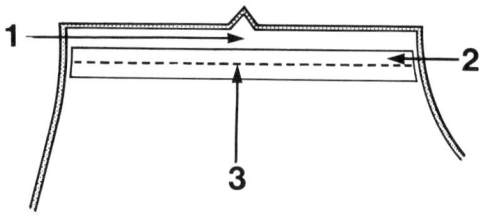

(ii) Why is it necessary to stabilize the shoulder seams of this garment?

(iii) Give details for pressing this seam when completed, using the fabric chosen in (d).

a. Study the outfit illustrated above and describe the fashion features of the jacket and pinafore dress.

b. Name the five main pattern pieces. What other pieces would be needed to make these garments?

48

Question 44

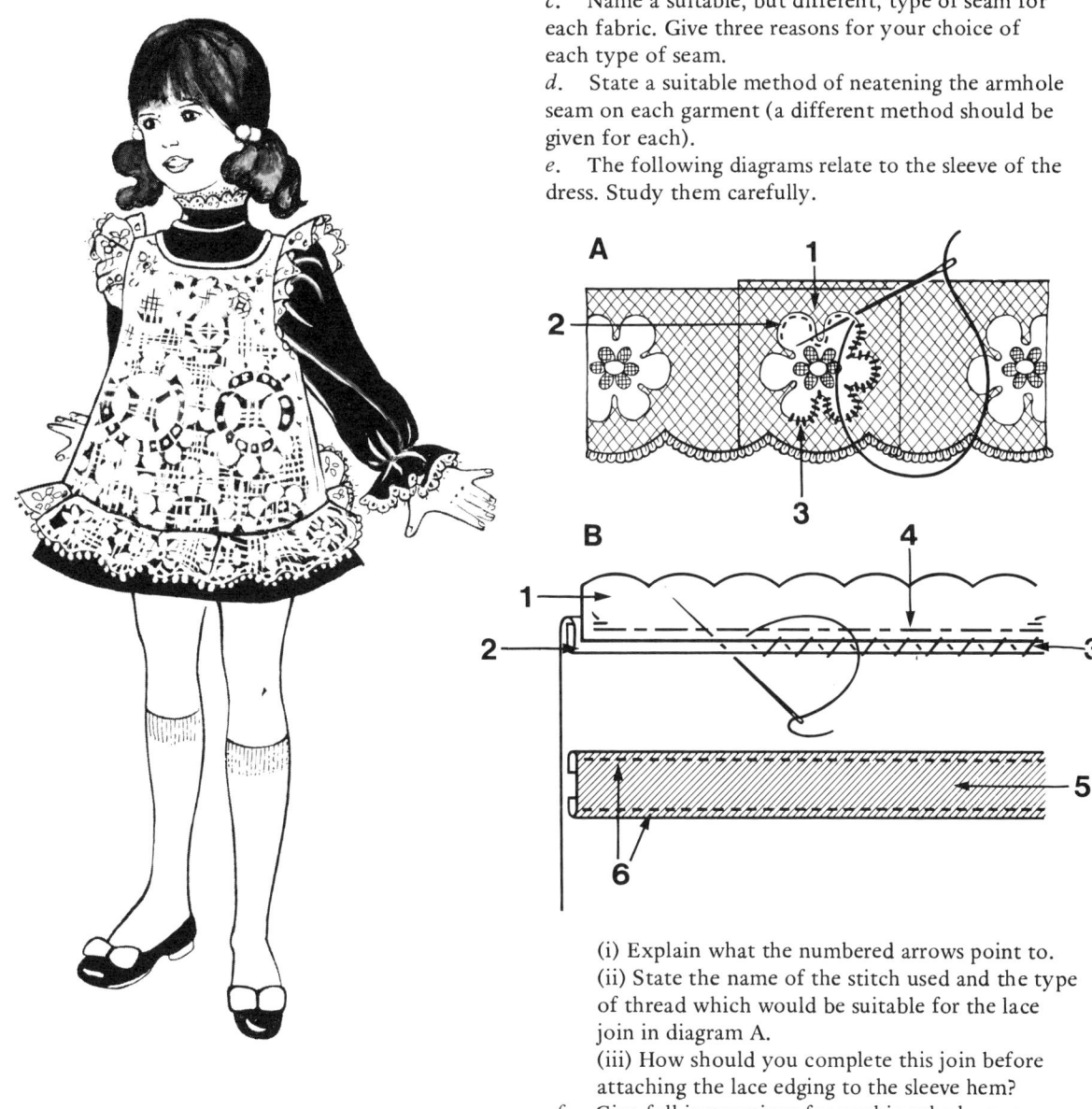

c. Name a suitable, but different, type of seam for each fabric. Give three reasons for your choice of each type of seam.

d. State a suitable method of neatening the armhole seam on each garment (a different method should be given for each).

e. The following diagrams relate to the sleeve of the dress. Study them carefully.

(i) Explain what the numbered arrows point to.

(ii) State the name of the stitch used and the type of thread which would be suitable for the lace join in diagram A.

(iii) How should you complete this join before attaching the lace edging to the sleeve hem?

f. Give full instructions for washing the lace apron.

a. Name and describe a suitable fabric for each garment of the child's outfit illustrated above.

b. What four qualities would you look for when selecting these fabrics?

Question 45

From each of the following groups of terms, select the odd one out and give a reason for your choice:

a. Polyester, Polyamide, Acrylic, Nylon.
b. Natural, Regenerated, Chemical, Synthetic.
c. North Down, South Down, Merino, Crossbred.

d. Courtelle, Acrilan, Nylon, Orlon.
e. Tricel, Dicel, Viscose, Celon.
f. Silk, Rayon, Cotton, Wool.
g. Tricel, Vincel, Sarille, Evlan.
h. Nylon, Terylene, Orlon, Rayon.
i. Terylene, Dacron, Trevira, Tricel.
j. Jute, Flax, Hemp, Cotton.
k. Celon, Blue C, Orlon, Bri-nylon.

l. Sliver, Yarn, Filament, Staple fibre.
m. Reeling, Roving, Scouring, Carding.
n. Retting, Ginning, Carding, Spinning.
o. Spinneret, Sliver, Filament, Extrusion.

p. Jap, Shantung, Lawn, Tussore.
q. Plain, Hopsack, Twill, Tricot.
r. Stockinette, Tweed, Tricot, Jersey.
s. Velvet, Needlecord, Satin, Corduroy.
t. Viyella, Clydella, Tricelon, Worsted.
u. Shantung, Worsted, Gaberdine, Serge.

v. Block, Screen, Roller, Vat.
w. Mercerized, Glazed, Brushed, Calendered.
x. Sanforized, Rigmel, Dylan, Mitin.
y. Dyed, Printed, Batik, Tie and dye.

Right: Knee length dress in printed floral design in four colourways all on natural cheesecloth.

Question 46

a. Study the sketch of the dress and name the style features indicated by the numbered arrows. Draw a sketch of the back view of the dress showing the style details.

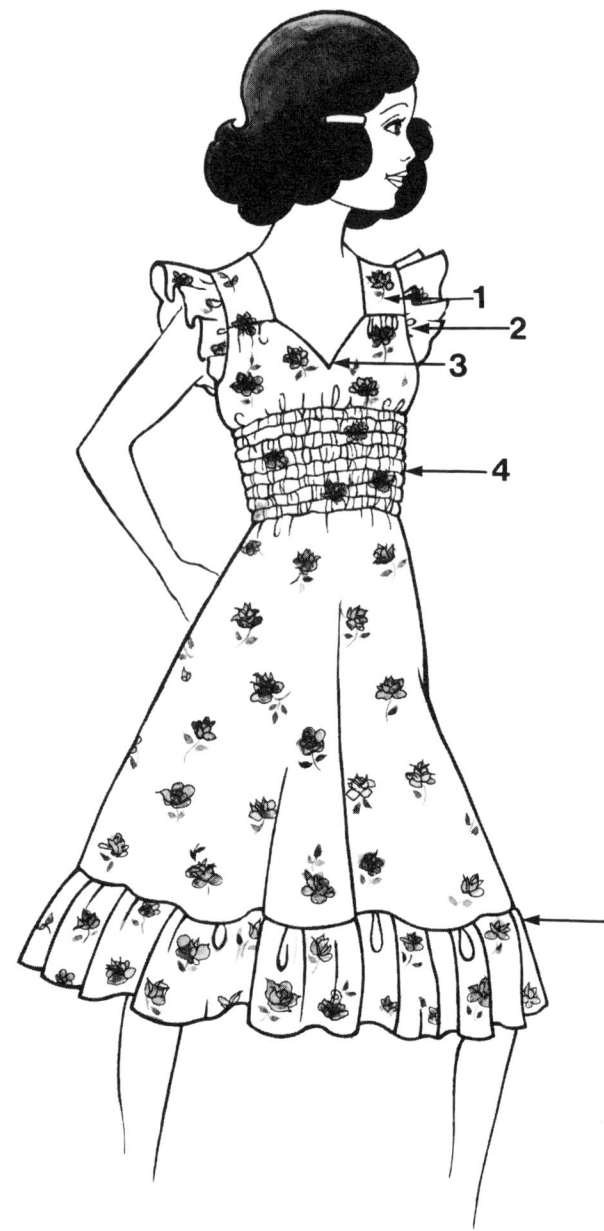

b. (i) The description of the dress says 'Printed floral design'. Give words to complete the spaces in the sentences below, which describe the printing of this fabric.

The _____ fabric is fed through _____ copper_____, one for each _____. Each has _____ blades, one to _____ off surplus paste, the _____ to remove_____. Below is another _____ which collects the colour from a _____ underneath.

(ii) Name four types of roller printing.

(iii) Explain what is meant by 'Four colourways'. Give examples.

c. The dress is made from natural cheesecloth. Describe this fabric.

d. Name two methods of disposing of fullness used in this dress.

e. How would you ensure that the rows of machining on the midriff section were:

(i) In the correct position as on the pattern,

(ii) Equidistant from each other?

f. The frill is neatened by the self binding method. Explain the numbered arrows on the following diagrams to show that you understand fully the working of this method.

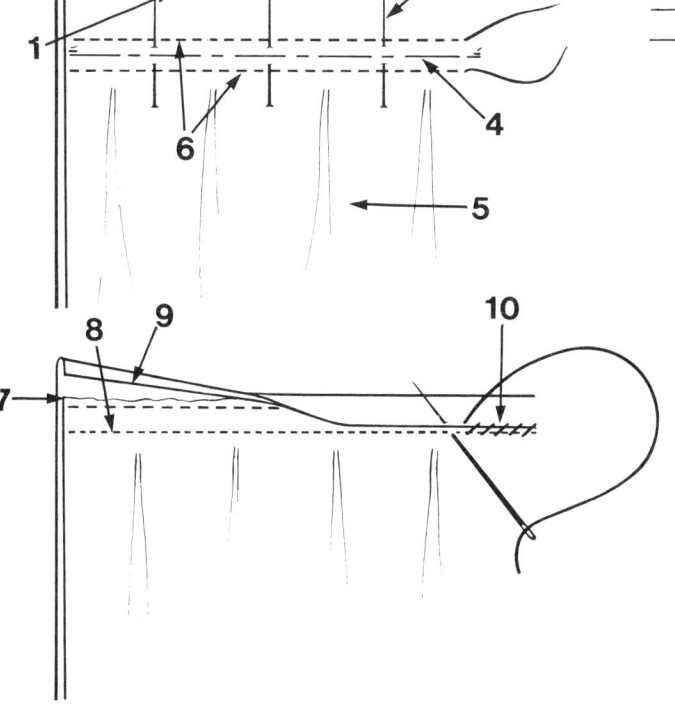

Question 47

Refer to the sketch in Question 46(a).

a. (i) List the pattern pieces which would be required for this dress.

(ii) Underline the pieces which would be placed to the fold in the layout.

b. This dress does not need a back opening. Give reasons why this is so.

c. Name five stitches which would be worked by hand during the making of this dress. State where and why each stitch would be used.

d. The dress could be made of Terylene lawn. Give words to complete the following explanation for the working of the elasticated midriff section of the dress when using this fabric.

Complete the _____ seams and_____ with a _____ iron. Wind _____ elastic _____ and evenly on to a _____. Thread the machine with _____ and select a _____ stitch._____ machine on a scrap of_____ fabric the _____ as the dress. Working on the _____ side of the dress, begin at one _____ _____ and machine round the dress carefully following the tacks. Leave_____ ends. Work other rows _____ and _____ spaced. Remove _____ and finish off the ends of _____ and thread very _____.

Question 48

Refer to the sketch in question 46(a).

a.   You could use Terylene lawn for making this dress.

　　(i) Describe the fabric.

　　(ii) List the notions you would need. In each case give the quantity and type.

　　(iii) State the size of machine stitch and machine needle to be used.

　　(iv) What type and size of hand sewing needle should be used?

b.   (i) Explain the preparation of the neck facing so that it is ready to apply to the neckline as in the diagram below.

　　(ii) How would you deal with the sections numbered 1, 2 and 3 to make sure that the facings were invisible when turned to the W.S.?

　　(iii) Why is there one stitch across the bottom of the 'V' at 4?

c.   The seam joining the frill to the skirt could be self bound. Name four other possible methods of neatening this seam. In which direction should it be pressed?

d.   Describe how you could finish off the lower edge of the skirt frill in the following circumstances:

　　(i) If no machine were available, (ii) If a hand machine were available, (iii) If a fully automatic machine were available.

Question 49

a.   The diagram below shows the marking of the buttonhole positions for a garment.

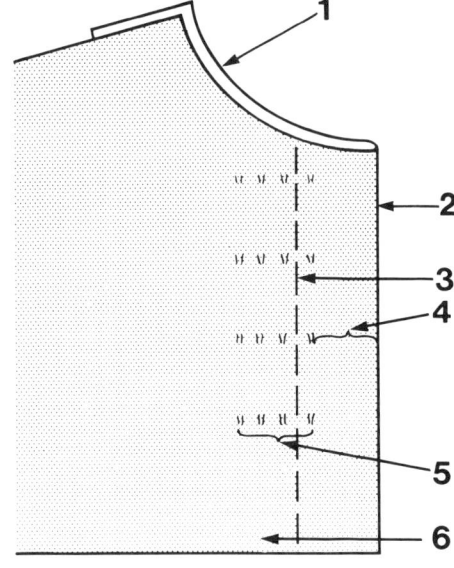

How are the buttonholes marked on the fabric? Explain the arrows as numbered to show that you understand the diagram.

b.   (i) What size binding strip would you cut out for a bound buttonhole to fit a 20-mm button?

　　(ii) State the grain of the binding strip.

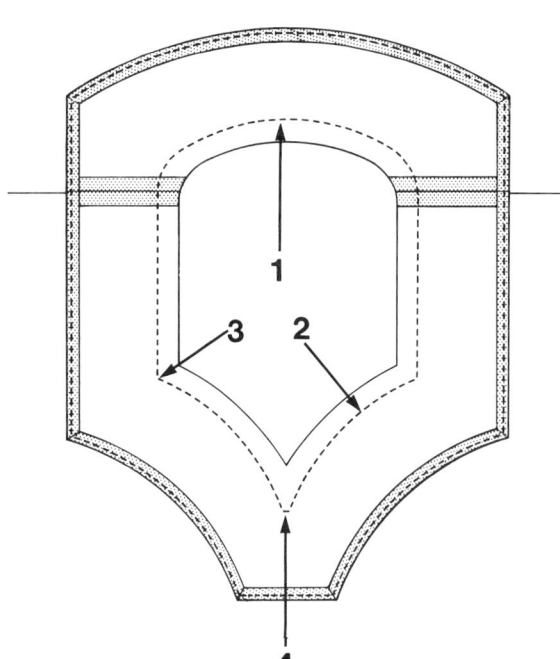

c.   The following diagrams show eight stages in making a bound buttonhole. For each stage write brief notes to explain the process.

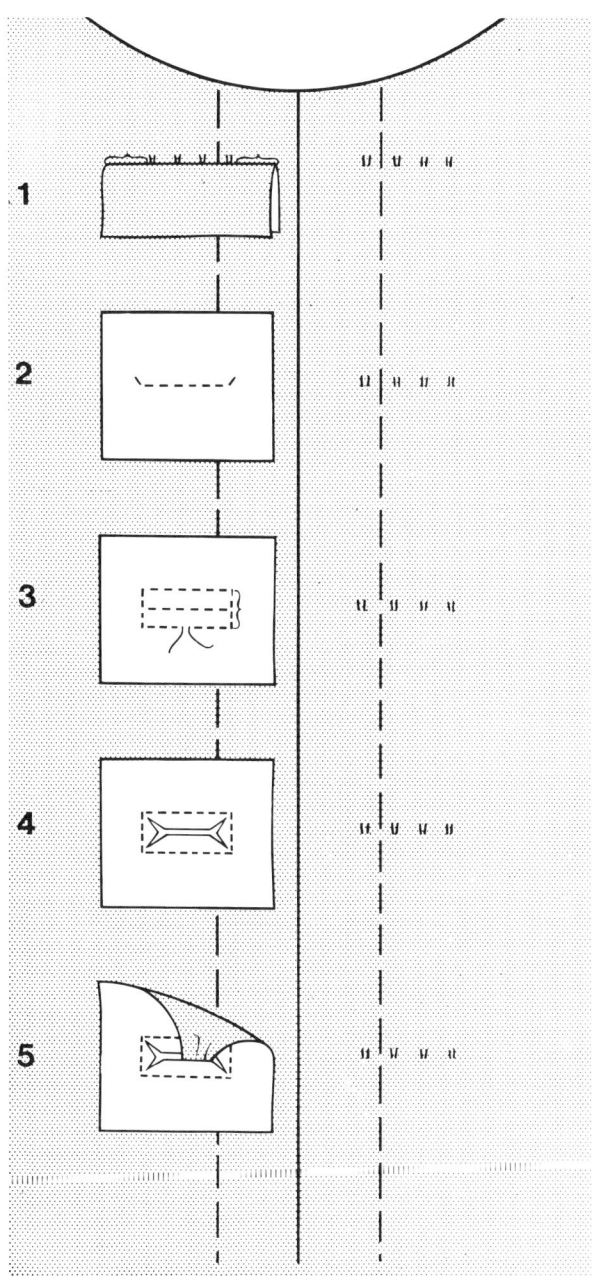

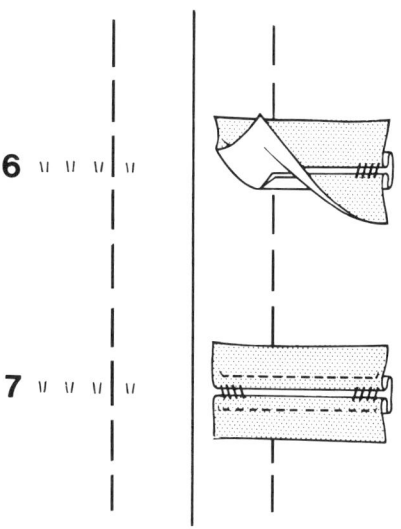

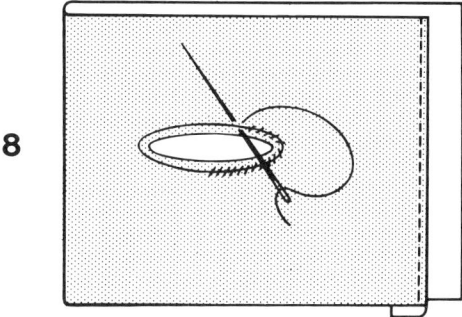

Question 50

a. (i) Study the sleeves numbered 1 to 7 and give the correct name for each one, using at least two words in each case.

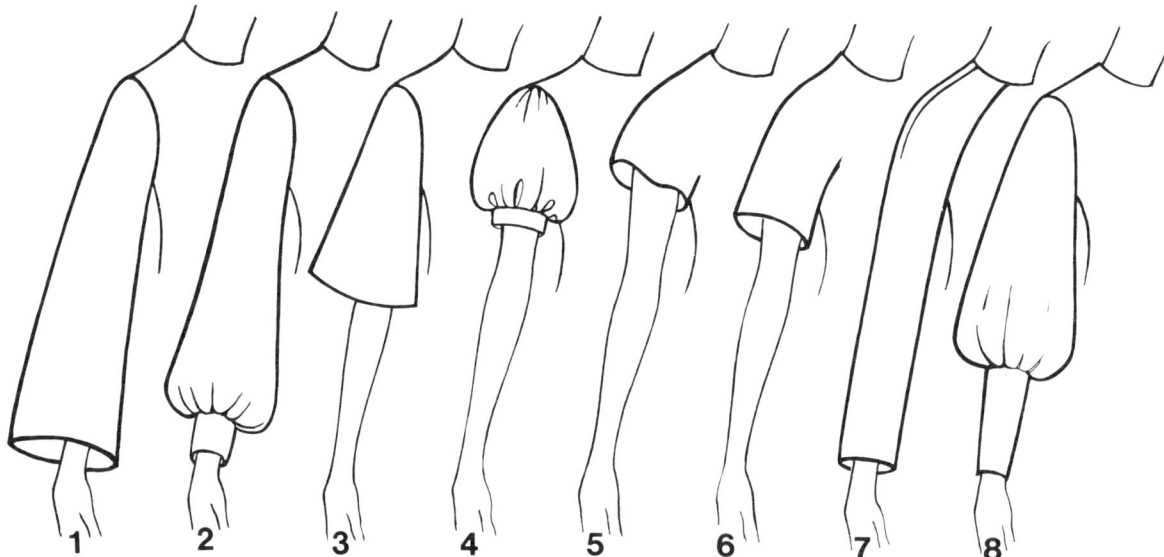

(ii) Name the feature which sleeves 1 to 4 have in common.

(iii) What have sleeves 1 to 3 in common?

b. Trace the outline of this pattern for sleeve 2. On your tracing:

(i) Draw the straight grain arrow, notches, balance points, fitting line, lengthening or shortening line and position for the easing threads.

(ii) Label the back, front and crown.

(iii) Mark the opening position and state its length.

c. (i) Show by clearly labelled diagrams how the pattern for sleeve 2 could be altered to make sleeve 8.

(ii) Give details for the adaptation of the cuff. Draw the finished cuff pattern complete with all markings.

Question 51

a. (i) Study the diagrams below and give a full description of each wrist finish.

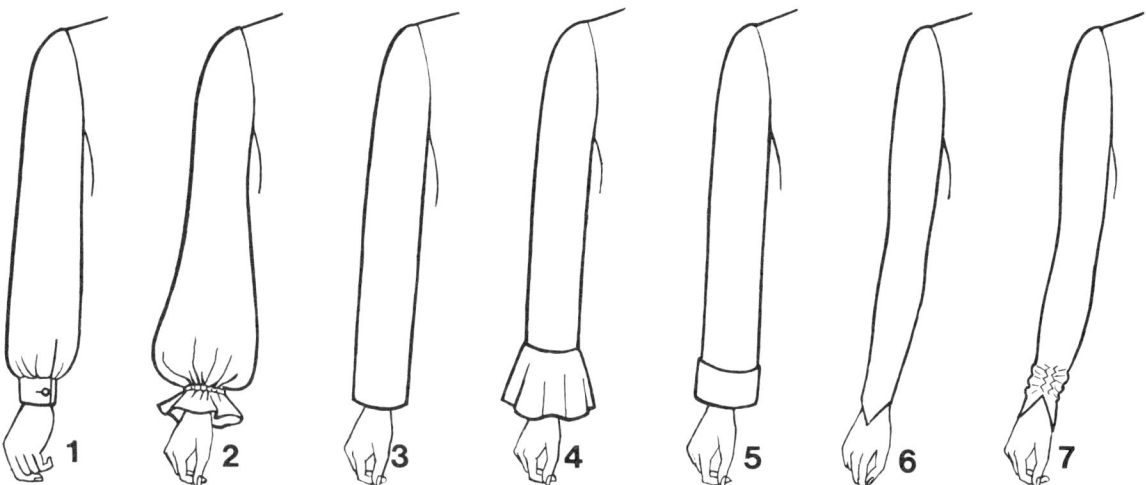

(ii) Suggest a different style of garment and type of fabric for each of the above wrist finishes.

b. Make a sketch of the shape of the pattern pieces which would be required for wrist finishes 1, 4 and 6.

c. Explain in detail how to work finish 7.

Question 52

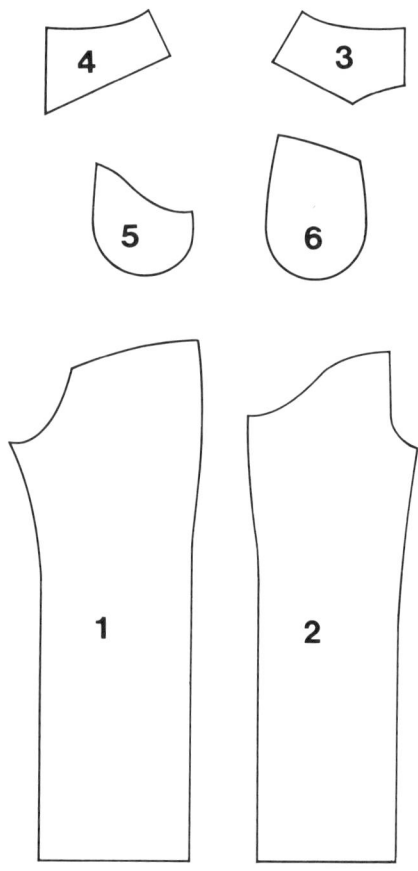

a. Study the sketch and the pattern pieces above.
(i) Name the pattern pieces for the trousers.
(ii) Name and describe the appearance of a
suitable type of fabric (150 cm wide) for this
garment and give three reasons for your choice.

b. Draw a rectangle to represent the 150 cm wide
fabric. Mark the fold and selvedges. Trace and cut
out the pattern pieces 1, 2, 3, 4 and 6 given above and
use them to help you plan a layout for the trousers.

c. (i) Pieces 3 and 4 will be lined and 5 will be cut
from the lining fabric. Name and describe a
suitable lining fabric 90 cm wide and give reasons
for your choice.
(ii) State the approximate length of lining required and say how you would estimate this.
(iii) List the other items which would be required
to complete the trousers. For each item state the
quantity, type and size required.

Question 53

a. Name and describe a suitable type of fabric for the child's dress illustrated. Give four reasons for your choice.

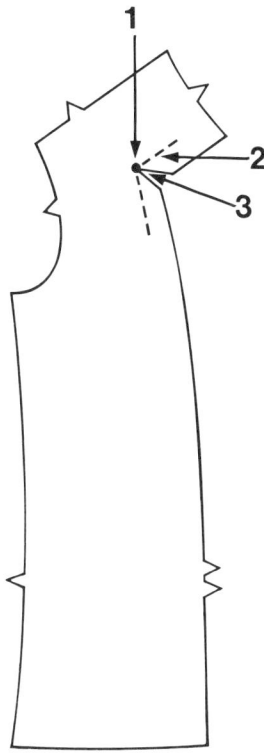

b. This is the shape of the side front of the dress.
(i) Explain the diagram showing the three stages for treating the corner of the side front before assembling the garment. Give a reason in each case.
(ii) How would you neaten the seam joining this section of the dress to the centre front panel?
(iii) In which direction should the finished seam be pressed?

c. The following machine and hand sewn stitches are used in the making of this dress before making and applying the bows. Give one position for each stitch and a reason for using it:
(i) Ease stitching, (ii) Stay stitching, (iii) Understitching, (iv) Hemming, (v) Slip hemming.

d.   (i) How much ribbon would be needed to make the two decorative bows?
(ii) Name a suitable type and width of ribbon for the bows.
(iii) The first two instructions for making the bows are given below:

1.   Cut off two 3.8 cm strips for the knots.
2.   Cut the remaining ribbon into two equal parts.
Describe the diagrams showing stages 3, 4 and 5 to complete the instructions for making a bow.

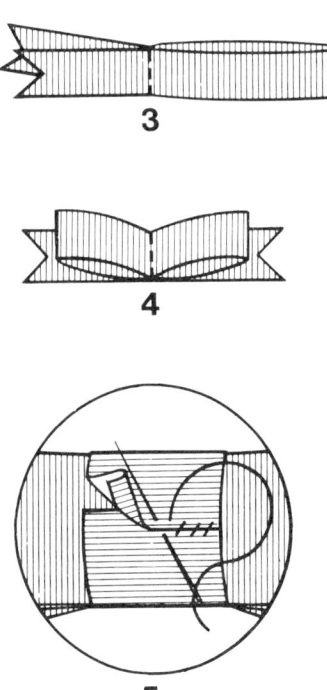

(iv) Why are the raw ends cut to the shape shown?
(v) Give two reasons why the bows might be attached to the dress by press studs.

Question 54

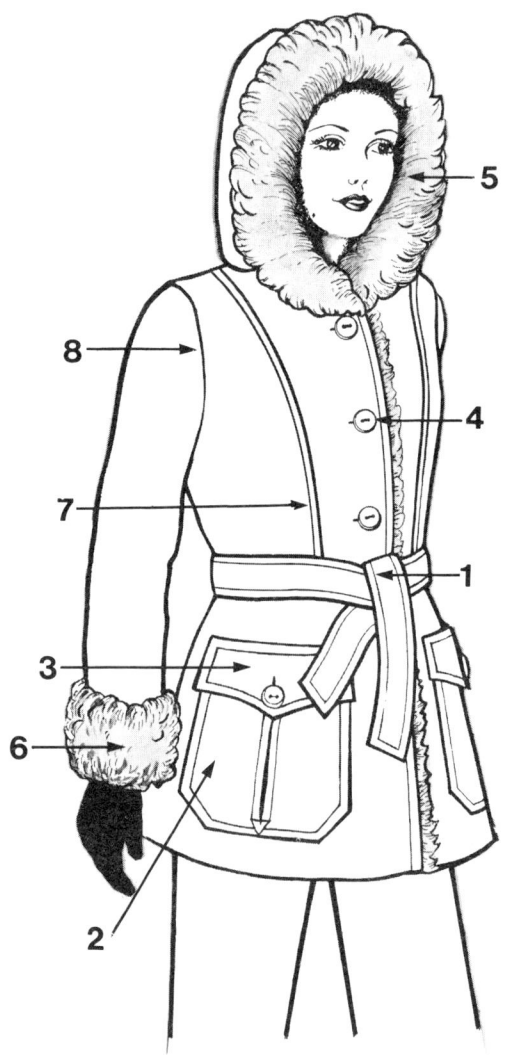

a.   Study the sketch and name the style features as indicated by the numbered arrows.
b.   Suggest and describe a suitable fabric for the jacket.

c. What points should you consider before purchasing to ensure that the jacket is:
    (i) A good buy,
    (ii) A good fit?

d. What advantages does a lined jacket offer?

e. Give instructions in note form for the removal of an oil mark from the elbow of the jacket. State the agent to be used.

f. Explain the following symbols which might be found on the label of a jacket like this.

A   B   C   D   E

Question 55

Refer to the jacket sketch in Question 54.

When this jacket was purchased there were no belt carriers. You decide to make some by shortening the belt and using the fabric which you have cut off.

a. Explain how to shorten the belt and how to finish the end of it to look like new.

b. Give details for preparing the piece of belt to make the belt carriers.

c. (i) How do you decide how long the pieces of fabric for the carriers should be?
    (ii) State the size of the pieces and the position of the straight grain.

d. Study the diagrams below showing how the carriers are made. Explain the diagrams as indicated by the numbered arrows and explain how the raw edges (6) are neatened.

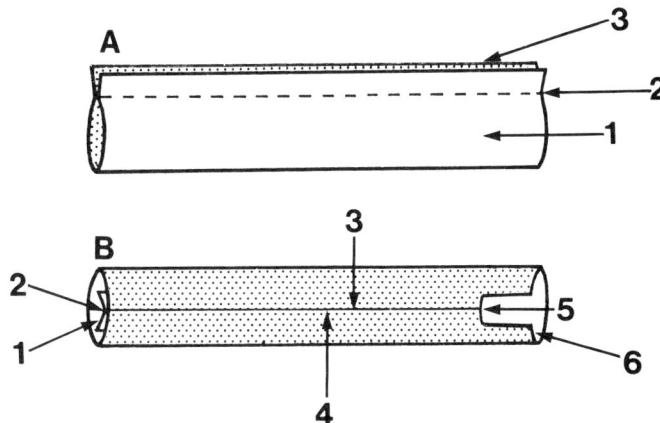

e. Explain how to determine the correct position for the carriers.

f. Give instructions for attaching a carrier in the correct position.

g. How would you replace a button which had come off the jacket?

Question 56

Instruction sheets given with commercial patterns are a great help to the home dressmaker, but important details are often omitted.

a. Study the diagram and instructions below for inserting a sleeve.

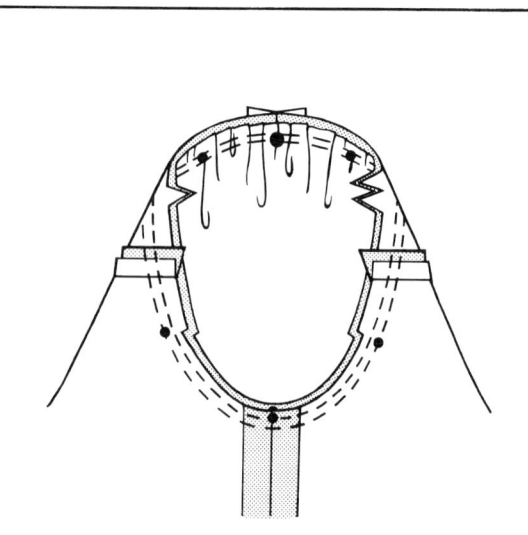

With right sides together, pin sleeve in armhole, placing large ● at shoulder seam. Adjust gathers. Stitch. Stitch again 6 mm away in seam allowance. Trim seam below small ●s close to stitching. Press. Turn seam toward sleeve.

(i) List fifteen important details which are omitted from the instructions and which would be most helpful to a beginner.

(ii) List four details omitted from the diagram.

b. List the equipment you would need to press the completed armhole seam.

c. Give the iron setting required for the following fabrics:

(i) Cotton poplin, (ii) Neospun jersey, (iii) Afgalaine, (iv) Dacron lawn.

d. For each of the above fabrics state a different method of neatening the armhole seam.

e. The diagrams below show the method to be followed when completing the hem of a tunic. Study the diagrams and make a complete list of suitable instructions for a pattern sheet (twelve points).

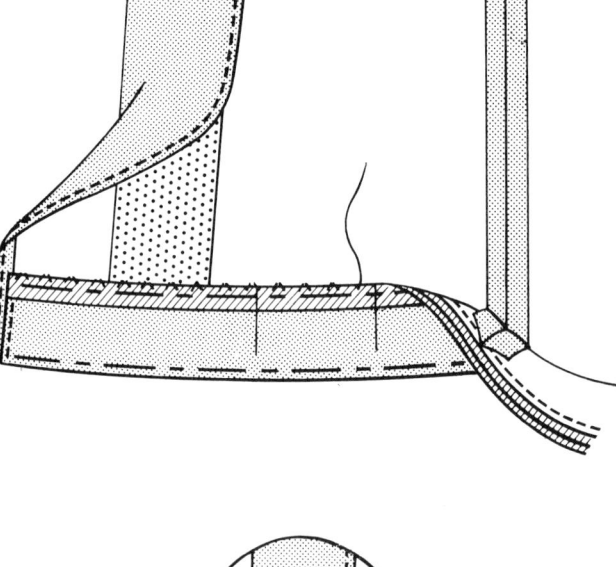

f. Draw working diagrams (two stages) of the stitch used to fix the hem. Name the stitch.

g. Suggest another method of neatening the hem edge.

Question 57

The following are all fabric finishes:

1. Mitin
2. Proban
3. Sanforized
4. Mercerized
5. Trubenized

6. Tebilized
7. Anti-stat
8. Acti-fresh
9. Silicone
10. Brushed

a. From the above list select the appropriate finish to give the following effects on the fabric:

crease resistance
shower proof
warmth
flame proof
lustre

bacteria resistance
moth proof
resistance to 'static'
shrink resistance
permanently stiff

b. For each finish name a fabric which could be so treated.

c. Name two articles of clothing for which each finish is desirable.

Question 58

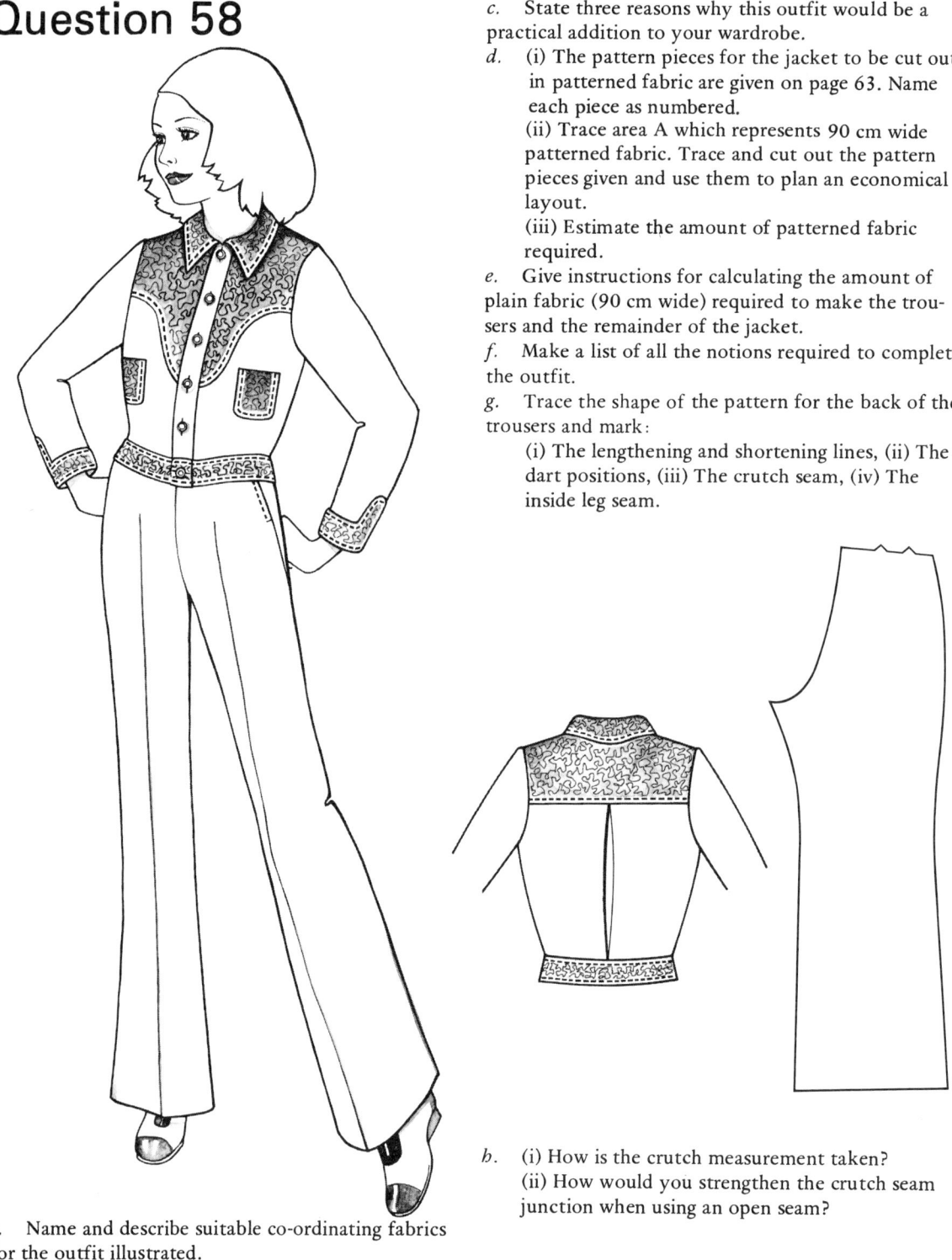

c. State three reasons why this outfit would be a practical addition to your wardrobe.

d. (i) The pattern pieces for the jacket to be cut out in patterned fabric are given on page 63. Name each piece as numbered.

(ii) Trace area A which represents 90 cm wide patterned fabric. Trace and cut out the pattern pieces given and use them to plan an economical layout.

(iii) Estimate the amount of patterned fabric required.

e. Give instructions for calculating the amount of plain fabric (90 cm wide) required to make the trousers and the remainder of the jacket.

f. Make a list of all the notions required to complete the outfit.

g. Trace the shape of the pattern for the back of the trousers and mark:

(i) The lengthening and shortening lines, (ii) The dart positions, (iii) The crutch seam, (iv) The inside leg seam.

h. (i) How is the crutch measurement taken?

(ii) How would you strengthen the crutch seam junction when using an open seam?

a. Name and describe suitable co-ordinating fabrics for the outfit illustrated.

b. Give four reasons for your choice of fabrics.

A

B

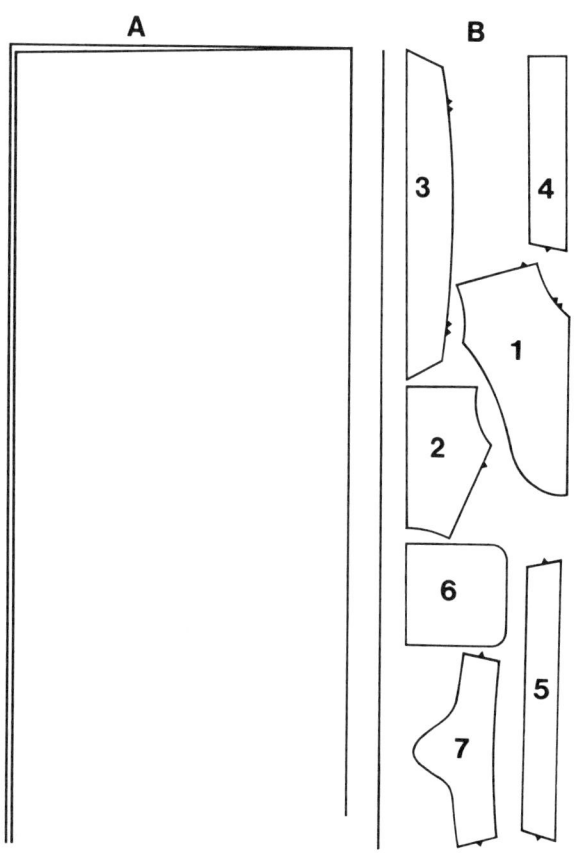

Question 59

Refer to the outfit illustrated in Question 58.

a. This is the shape of the pattern for the waistband of the trousers. Name and state the use of ten pattern markings illustrated on the pattern piece.

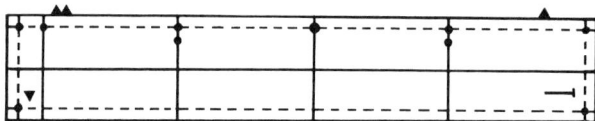

b. The seam illustrated below could be used for the trousers. Name it and explain the arrows as numbered to show that you understand how the seam is made.

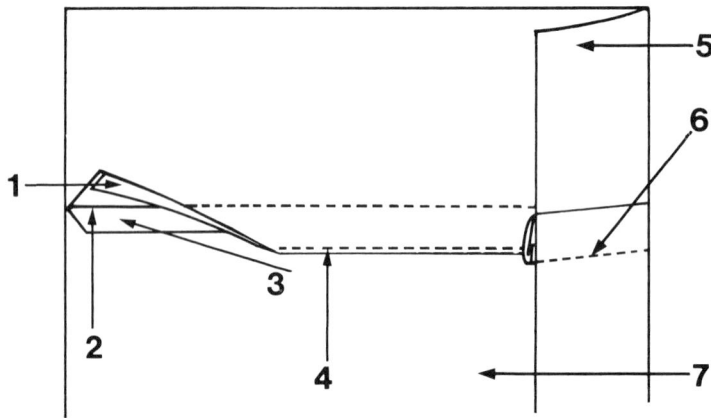

c. You accidentally make a hole in the knee of the trousers and decide to patch it with the patterned fabric for strength and decoration.

(i) Name the type of patch illustrated.

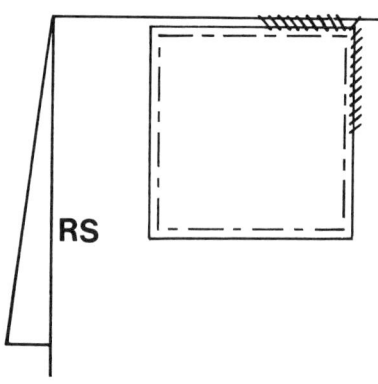

(ii) Make a copy of the stitches shown in the diagrams for working the patch. Draw the needle and thread in position for the next stitch. Name each stitch.

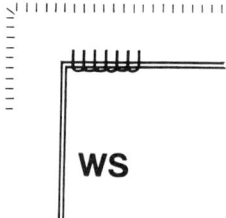

(iii) Give details of another suitable, but quicker, method of repair for these trousers.

d. The jacket will be made by unit construction. What does this mean? List the units which will be followed for the jacket.

Question 60

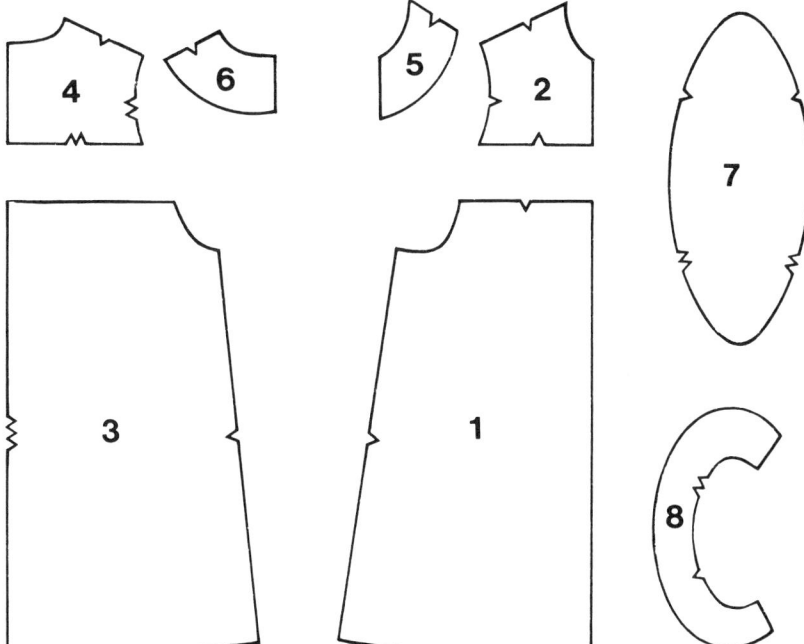

a. With the aid of the child silhouette on the inside back cover, sketch the front and back views of the dress that would be made by using the eight pattern pieces shown above.

b. Name the pattern pieces as numbered.

c. If you had insufficient fabric to cut piece number 7 as shown, how could you alter this to give the same finished effect?

d. On re-using the pattern, you find you have mislaid pieces 5 and 6. Show by diagrams how you could make your own pattern pieces.

e. Trace pattern pieces 1 and 3 and on these outlines draw the pattern markings shown below in the appropriate places. Name the pattern markings shown.

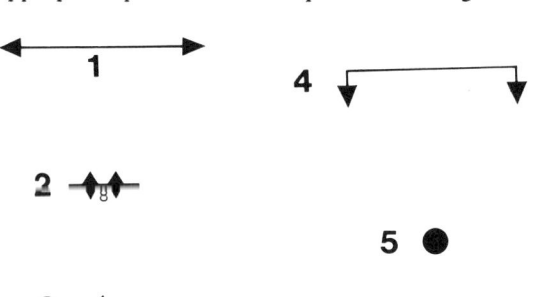

f. What do the following indicate on a pattern piece?

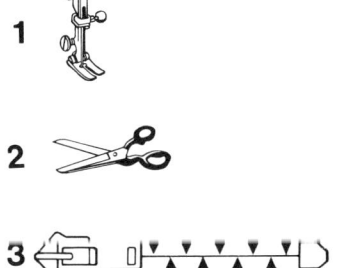

g. State the three points you should consider when selecting the layout.

Question 61

a. Supply words to fill in the spaces in the following sentences:

Buttons must be sewn on _____ fabric. If it is _____ it must be _____ with a stay. The _____ edges of the _____ must be _____ . Buttons are _____ on _____ buttonholes are made, but before _____ are made. A _____ is necessary _____ the _____ and the _____ to allow the fabric to remain _____ when the _____ is _____ . Shanks may be _____ on to the _____ or _____ whilst _____ it on. The _____ the fabric the _____ the shank needs to be. The button should be _____ on with _____ thread of a suitable _____ and _____ .

b. (i) Diagrams A and B below show two different methods of applying a button stay. State a fabric for which each method would be suitable and suggest a different position on a garment for each one.

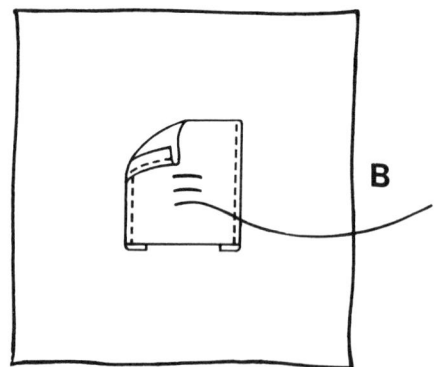

(ii) Name five materials suitable for making a button stay.

c. Study diagrams C and D showing two front openings. Explain the numbered arrows and show that you understand how the position of the button is found.

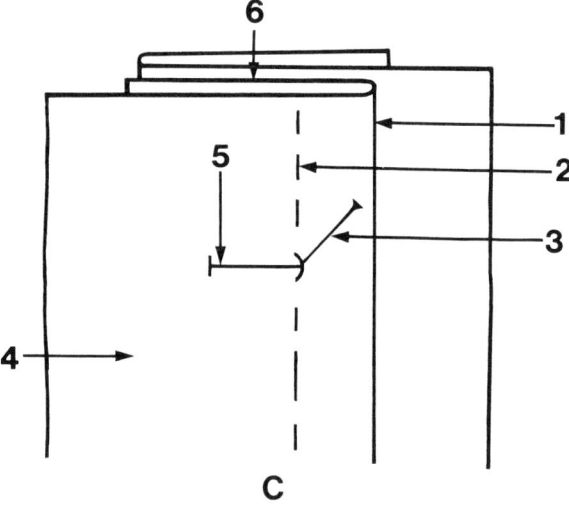

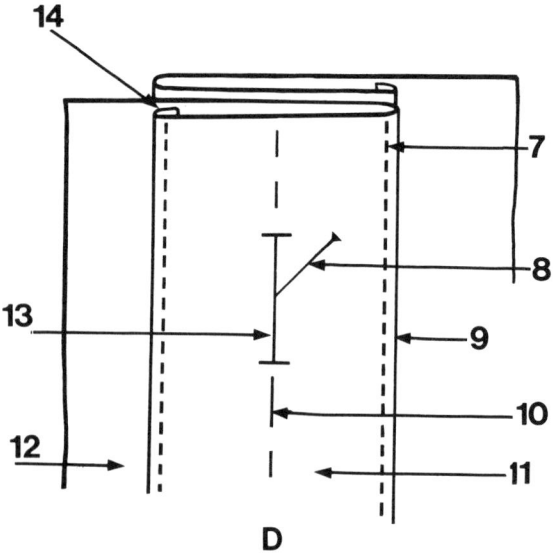

Question 62

Refer to diagrams C and D in Question 61.

a. Giving reasons, explain the differences between the two buttonholes illustrated.

b. (i) Name the method of opening illustrated in D and write tabulated instructions for working it.
(ii) Name two fabrics which would be suitable for this type of opening. Give a reason.

c. Illustrate a section of a pattern piece for a garment with this type of front opening. Label clearly.

d. Give words to complete the spaces in this paragraph about bound buttonholes.

Bound buttonholes are _____ satisfactory for _____ garments as the _____ are _____ in construction and therefore _____ out if _____ washed. The buttonholes are worked on _____ fabric and _____ on the _____ side by the garment _____ . They are made _____ in the construction of the _____ _____ the _____ is fixed by a collar or _____ .

Question 63

a. Study the sketch and describe the style details as indicated by the numbered arrows.

b. Name the type of opening used at the C.F.

c. Estimate the amount of 90 cm wide fabric required for the blouse, showing clearly how you arrive at your answer.

d. Name and describe a suitable type of fabric for the blouse, giving four reasons for your choice.

e. Suggest a suitable type and width of braid for the decoration.

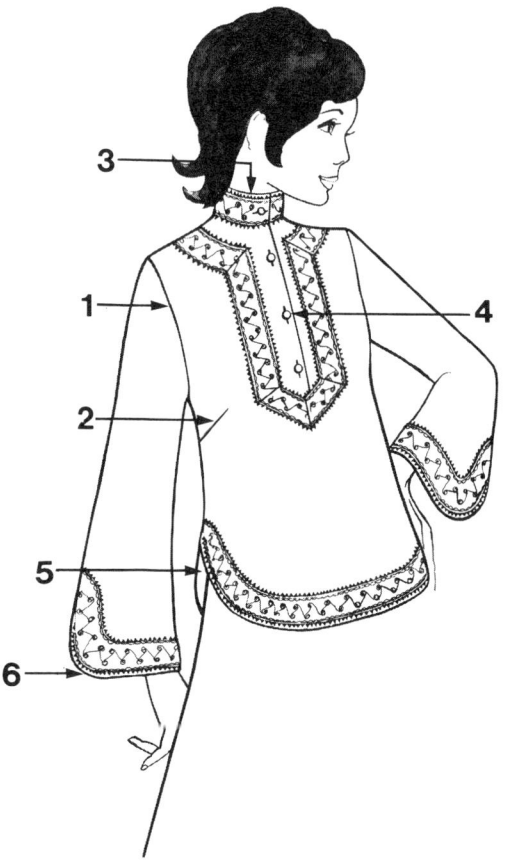

f. This diagram shows how to deal with the corners of the braid at the C.F. Explain the diagram carefully.

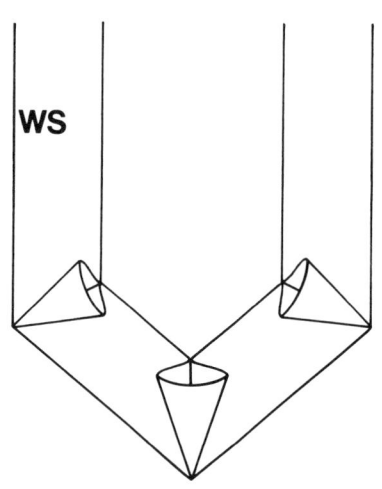

g. (i) Referring to diagrams below, describe how to sew on a button.

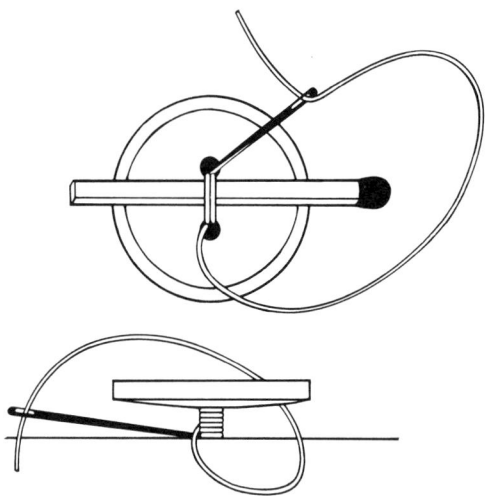

(ii) How should the W.S. be finished off? Illustrate your answer with a diagram.

h. (i) The buttonhole on the neckband will be horizontal and those at the C.F. vertical. If these buttonholes are worked by hand they should differ in style. How will they differ and why?
(ii) Make a clear working diagram of buttonhole stitch.

Question 64

Pockets may be cut as part of a garment.
a. Study the diagrams and supply the appropriate words to complete the details for making this type of pocket.
If a thick fabric is being used for the garment the pocket _____ should be cut from the _____ to _____ bulk.

Diagram A

Place _____ of _____ to _____ of garment. _____ and machine on the _____ _____ . Remove tackings, layer and _____ the _____ .

Diagram B

Mark _____ of pocket edge on the _____ by _____ .

Diagram C

Turn _____ to _____ rolling _____ slightly to _____ , _____ in position and _____ stitch. Remove _____ and _____ . With _____ sides uppermost, place _____ edge over the _____ matching _____ _____ , pin and _____ .

Diagram D

Turn to _____ , _____ and tack _____ to pocket _____ , making sure it is absolutely _____ . Machine on _____ _____ , remove _____ .

Diagram E

Trim _____ _____ to _____ and _____ with _____ stitch.
b. (i) State a type of fabric for which the method of neatening shown in diagram E is suitable.
(ii) Give three different types of fabric which could be used for the garment and which would each need a different method of neatening the pocket bag. In each case state the method of neatening you would use.
(iii) Name two suitable types of lining for the pocket facing which could be used with the fabric stated in *b*(i).

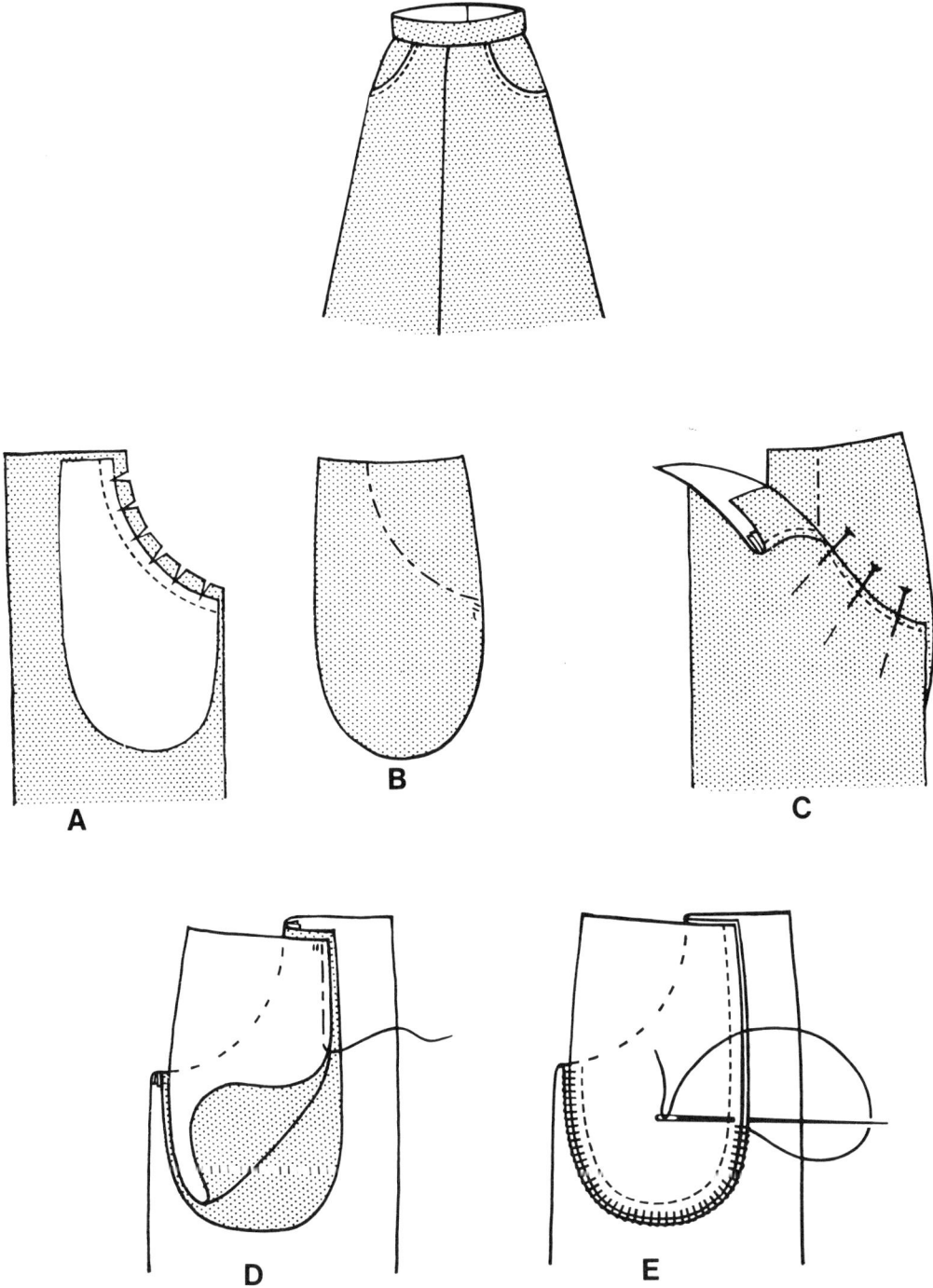

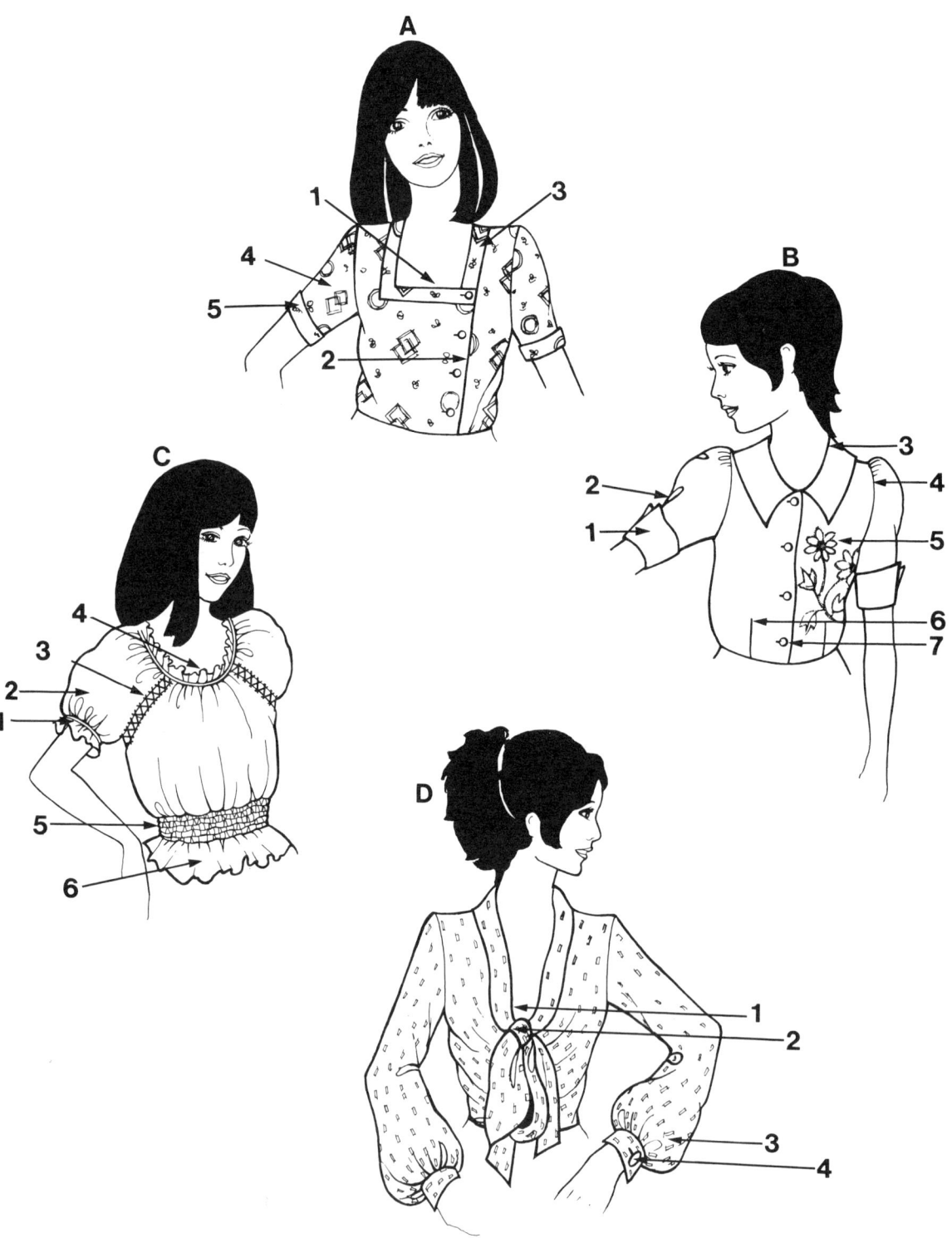

Question 65

a. Study blouse A illustrated on page 70 and describe fully the style features indicated by the numbered arrows.

b. This blouse could be made in printed Tricelon pongee. Describe each aspect of this fabric.

c. (i) Suggest a suitable type of interfacing to be used with this fabric and state three positions where it could be used.
(ii) Give full details of the notions required to complete this blouse.

d. The pattern for this blouse could be adapted to make a tennis dress. Giving reasons state:
(i) Two style features which would be retained,
(ii) Two adaptations which would be advisable,
(iii) The name of a fabric which would be particularly suitable for the tennis dress.

Question 66

a. Study blouse B illustrated on page 70 and describe fully the style features indicated by the numbered arrows.

b. This blouse could be made from tricel georgette. Describe this fabric.

c. (i) Copy part of the motif which is on the blouse and give full details of the stitches, thread(s) and colour(s) which you would use for working it. At least three different stitches should be shown.
(ii) State the type and size of needle you would use for the embroidery.
(iii) Make working diagrams of two of the stitches you have shown.

d. Give words to complete the following sentences: If the blouse was made in a sheer fabric the motif could be adapted for _____ work by making a _____ petal inside the original ones, keeping the _____ the same. Treat the _____ in a similar manner, the veins could be worked in _____ stitch. The stitch used for this type of work is _____ _____ and the embroidery is worked on the _____ side.

Question 67

Refer to the sketch of blouse B on page 70.

a.   Name the five main pattern pieces which would be needed for this blouse.

b.   List the correct order of working to be followed when commencing to make this blouse, as far as completing the cutting out.

c.   For each piece of pattern stated in (*a*), list all the markings which would need transferring to the fabric.

d.   (i) Name two different methods for applying the collar.

   (ii) Give brief details for two methods of attaching the cuffs. These should be different from those given in (i) for attaching the collar.

e.   When using this blouse pattern for a second time you decide to change the style of the collar into a 'Peter Pan' and the sleeve into a puffed one with a straight band 3 cm wide. Trace the outlined diagrams of the original pattern pieces given here and show clearly the alterations you would make.

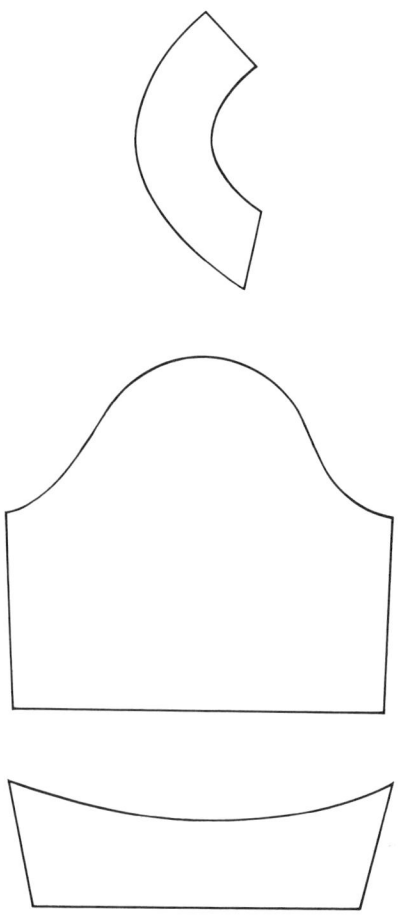

Question 68

a. Study blouse C illustrated on page 70 and describe fully the style features indicated by the numbered arrows.
b. This blouse could be made from printed drip-dry cotton with a very small design. List seven qualities of this fabric which make it suitable for this gipsy-style blouse.
c. Study the following diagram carefully. It shows the seven stages for working the decorative seam. Put these stages in the correct order for working and explain each one.

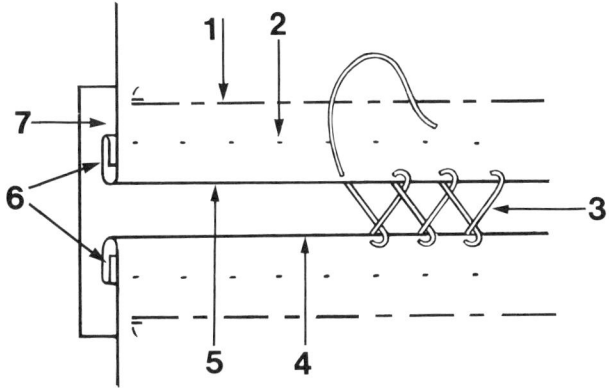

d. Draw a two-stage diagram showing how the stitch is worked.

Question 69

a. Study blouse D illustrated on page 70 and describe fully the style features indicated by the numbered arrows.
b. This blouse could be made from self-patterned crêpe de chine. Describe fully the appearance of this fabric.
c. (i) List the pattern pieces which would be needed to make this blouse.
    (ii) Underline the pattern pieces which should be cut twice on double fabric.
d. Bearing in mind the fabric given in (b), state:
    (i) The type of seam, (ii) The type of sleeve opening, (iii) The type of armhole neatening, (iv) The type of buttonhole you would recommend and give a different reason for each.
e. List the correct order of working (twenty-one stages) to be followed when making this blouse, after cutting out and transferring the pattern markings to the fabric.

Question 70

Turn to page 70 and study the four blouses illustrated. Each of these blouses could be worn with a simple skirt, but on different occasions. Dealing with each blouse separately and giving different answers in each case:
a. Describe the style features of a suitable, simple skirt to be worn with the blouse.
b. State an occasion on which the outfit could be worn.
c. Name and describe suitable accessories to wear with the outfit.

Answers 1-70

Answer 1

a. A. embroidery scissors (1); cutting threads (sewing and embroidery) (1)

    B. bent handled shears (3); cutting fabrics (1) 6

b. thumb, three, fingers, large, pointed, under, touching, left, flat, firmly, long, smooth 12

c. non-fray, non-stretch, metal ends, clearly marked, both sides marked 5

d.

	description	purpose	
(i)	ordinary length, round eye (2)	normal sewing (1)	
(ii)	shorter, round eye (2)	fine hand work (1)	
(iii)	ordinary length, oval eye (2)	embroidery (1)	
(iv)	no point, oval eye, thicker (2)	counted thread work (1)	12

e. Five other items (5) and two uses (10): sensible choice (zips, buttons, press studs, etc. not to be included; these should be purchased as required). 15

                                                     50

Answer 2

a. fastenings 1

b. 1 hook and eye, 2 hook and bar, 3 press stud, 4 button and worked loop 4

c. position on garment, edges meet or overlap, size of fastening, invisible or for decoration 4

d. 1 waist band, 2 under collar, 3 placket, 4 top of C.F. bound opening 4

e. (i) 1 tack position, 2 R.S., 3 edge tack, 4 pin to guide thread, 5 half diameter of button, 6 paper or card, 7 pins to show diameter of button (7)

(ii) hold edge towards you (1), fasten on securely, W.S. (1), pass needle through fold between pins (2), 4/5 strands over pin, back stitch to secure, remove pin (4), loop stitch over strands, closely, firmly, use eye of needle (5), first and last stitch through fabric, loops on outside (4), fasten off with double back stitch on W.S. (3)

(iii) worked bar: small, 3 strands, close to edge, no loop (4)

belt loop: larger, 6/7 strands, stronger, also flat (4)

positions worked loop: top of zip at back of dress (1)

                    belt loop: on side seam of dress, over the waistline (1) 37

                                                       50

Answer 3

a. (i) F.L. all round (2), dart size and shape (2), C.F. (1), S.G. (1), collar notch (1), shoulder notch ($\frac{1}{2}$), side notch ($\frac{1}{2}$), buttons and buttonholes even and level (4)   12
(ii) lengthening and shortening lines (1), name ($\frac{1}{2}$), size ($\frac{1}{2}$). pattern number ($\frac{1}{2}$), cut 2 (1), direction arrows ($\frac{1}{2}$)   4

e. (i) 2.5 cm (1), (ii) 6 mm (1), (iii) underarm, but not on the seam (2), (iv) hemming (1), (v) bias binding (1), (vi) fitted at waist, to make it wide enough to allow shoulders through (2)   8

$$\frac{}{50}$$

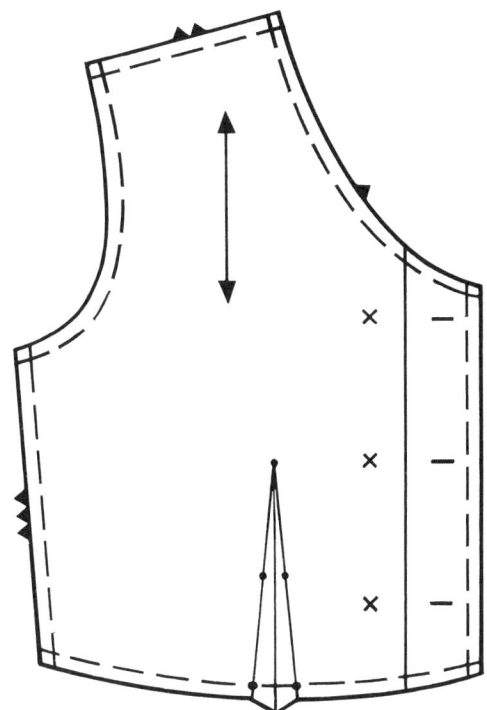

b. seam allowance armhole shaded (1) so that it is correct size when finished (1)   2

c. tailor tacks used for darts and buttonholes (1 + 2); tacking used for sides and shoulder (1 + 2); basting used for zip and collar (1 + 2)   9

d. A1 straight grain (1), warp/weft (1); A2 right-angled fold (1);   A3 fold on true cross (1)
B1 guide or marker (1);   B2 width or size of crossway (1);   B3 pins to mark (1)
C1 R.S. (1);   C2 W.S. (1);   C3 right angle (1);   C4 join (1)
D1 R.S. (1);   D2 R.S. (1);   D3 seam on straight grain (1);   D4 seam pressed open (cut points off) (1)   15

Answer 4

a. names and descriptions
A. bodkin: large eye, knob end (2)
B. stiletto: one very sharp pointed end with handle at other, made of bone or steel (2)
C. seam ripper (quick-unpick): sharp, shaped blade, bead to show extent (2)
D. tailor's chalk: white or coloured (black, red, blue, yellow), square or triangular. (2)

reasons for usefulness and examples
A blunt end for threading; ribbon, tape or elastic (2)
B threads not broken when piercing holes; eyelets in belt (2)
C very sharp cutting edge and slender point; unpicking incorrect machining, slitting machined buttonholes (2)
D clear marking on fabric which will stay until brushed off (white best as colours sometimes do not brush off); hemlines, dart positions, etc., use generally on W.S. (2)   16

b. (i) good fit for middle finger right (left) hand, metal (silver best), not too heavy, comfortable to wear, not smooth outside but no rough edges (4)
(ii) fine, sharp points, stainless, suitable length for fabric (4)   8

c. workmanship improves, speed of working improves, aids pushing in of needle, prevents sore finger end.   4

d. thick piece of card, cut out four notches; expect diagram (4)

e. heavy base, long ruler, marked both sides, adjustable, non-perishable tube and bulb, chalk holder and mouth or metal arms (non-rusting) with pin grooves   4

f. (i) three correct sizes (1 mark each), six correct fabrics ($\frac{1}{2}$ mark each)   6
(ii) check type of thread and stitch size (1), correct threading of upper and lower parts of machine (1), tension (1)   3
(iii) knitted and fine synthetics   1
          ——
          50

1.5 cm (seam allowance), 6 mm (French seam), 2.5 cm (cutting crossway), 9mm (French/double machined seams, etc.) (4)   8

Answer 5

a.	Tapestry	no point
b.	Sylko	cotton thread
c.	Accordian	commercial pleating
d.	Easing	small amount of fullness only (not to show)
e.	French knot	not a smocking stitch
f.	Wave	smocking stitch
g.	Oversewing	a joining stitch (rest neatening)
h.	Crew	neckline (rest collars)
i.	Puffed	set into armhole
j.	Peter Pan	collar (rest necklines)
k.	Household	patch (rest darns)
l.	Seam allowance	space (not a line)
m.	Raglan	not set-in (rest have armhole seams)
n.	'B'	no such thing (rest styles of dress)
o.	Crutch	trouser measure (rest on bodice)
p.	Kilt	not trousers
q.	Hip	not a dart position
r.	Thigh	not a skirt length
s.	Button	incomplete fastening
t.	Rouleau	made (rest are bought)
u.	Halter	not at waist
v.	Back waist	not a trouser measure
w.	Cutting line	does not help in making up
x.	Back waist	vertical measure
y.	Fitting line	does not help in layout

(25 x 2)   50
—
50

Answer 6

a. price, wood/metal, padded, size, shape, adjustable height, ease of storage, iron stand, etc. (any six)   6

b. sleeves, cuffs, sleeve seams, armhole seams, trouser leg seams, neck facings, shoulder seams, children's clothes (any five)   5

c. mitt on left (right) hand, padded side to knuckles, clench fist, blouse W.S. out, toe of iron into easing, press seam to armhole   6

d. Use rolling pin, piece of broom handle or tightly rolled newspaper. Pad with two layers of towelling and cover with cotton sheeting. Stitch on firmly.   3

e. (i) muslin; cotton, lightweight (old pillow case, etc.); linen, heavier weight (tea towel)
(ii) light fabrics and Courtelle; Crimplenes, medium wools, etc.; heavy woollen tweeds   6

f. voltage, weight, L.H. or R.H. flex-holder, BEAB mark, thermostat, shape of handle, sole plate shape, firmness when standing on its heel, indicator light, water level indicator   10

g. plug, flex, frayed, socket, switching, distilled (deionized), deposits (fur), sole, heat up, heel, empty, dry, heel, cool   14
—
50

Answer 7

a.   (i) all cotton fabrics and other washables
.(except as under) (4)
(ii) transparent fabrics, lawn, lace, velvet,
satin (4); wheel may damage fabric, coloured
mark may show through to R.S., pile may
be crushed (4)   **12**

b.   R.S., carbon, W.S., top, pin, pattern,
position, tracing wheel, lines, point   **11**

c.   tailor tacking (1); pattern and double fabric,
loop made with double thread (4); pattern
removed, pieces separated gently, cut in between (3); one layer of fabric marked with thread
(1)   **9**

d.   A. long and short tacking (1): *drawing*
needle in, out, thread from fabric, through
needle (3); inserting sleeve (firmer hold),
attaching collars (2)   **6**
B. even tacking (1): *drawing* as above (3);
marking centres and hemlines (2)   **6**
C. basting (1): *drawing* as above (3); holding
facings, collars, pleats (2)   **6**
(any sensible specific uses)

          50

Answer 8

a.   (3 + 3)   **6**

b.   *general points*
measurements to be taken by another
person, model to stand naturally, measurements to be taken over a thin garment, tape
not twisted, ease (two fingers under tape)
(any four points, 4)
details
bust: widest part; waist: natural; hip: widest
part; back waist: nape to waist; outside leg:
waist to length required (4)   **8**

c.   pattern size (1), type stated (1), pattern
measurements (4)   **6**

d.   bust (1): much easier to adjust hip/waist
than bodice as neckline, armholes, sleeves,
facings and collars are affected (2)   **3**

e.   Patterns allow ease for body movements
and style lines of garment. Without ease garments
would be tight, uncomfortable and unattractive.   **5**

f.   name (1); three sensible reasons (3), ('I like
it' will not do)   **4**

g.   (i) more than one garment: blouse, skirt,
jacket and trousers to be worn together;
good buy; better value (4)
(ii) quick to make; usually few pattern
pieces (2)
(iii) good for a beginner: directions usually
clear and without complicated processes (2)
(iv) woven fabrics must not be used; pattern
cut to give a closer fit (2)   **10**

h.   pattern (1), gift of fabric or a remnant
bought (2)   **3**

i.   Can I make it? Will it suit me? Is it economical? Is it made in my size? Is it a useful addition
to my wardrobe? (five sensible points)   **5**

          50

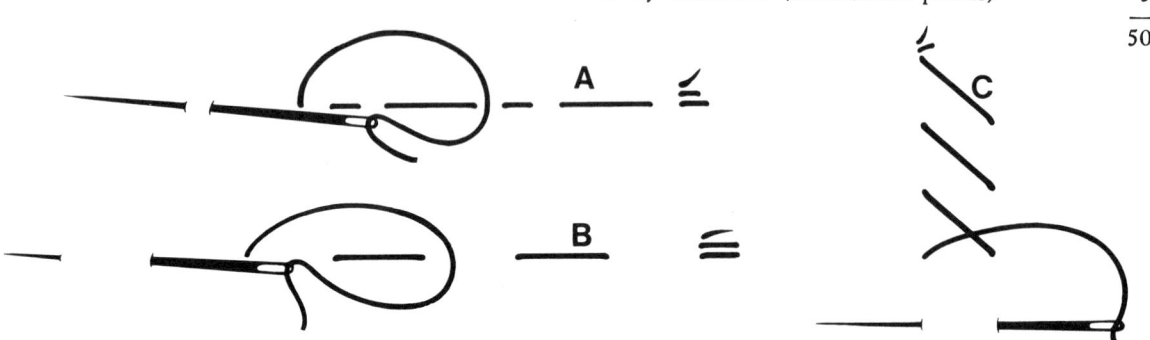

Answer 9

a. type of fabric, type of garment, position of
seam on garment   3
b.   A French seam, B Open seam   2
c. (i) e.g. Terylene lawn, cotton plissé (2)
     (ii) blouse: shoulder seam; nightdress:
     side seam (4)
     (iii) self neatening, wears well (2)   8
d. (i) diagrams (2 marks for each), name (1 mark
     for each), fabric (1 mark for each) (24)

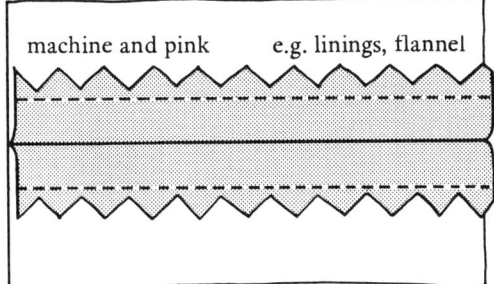

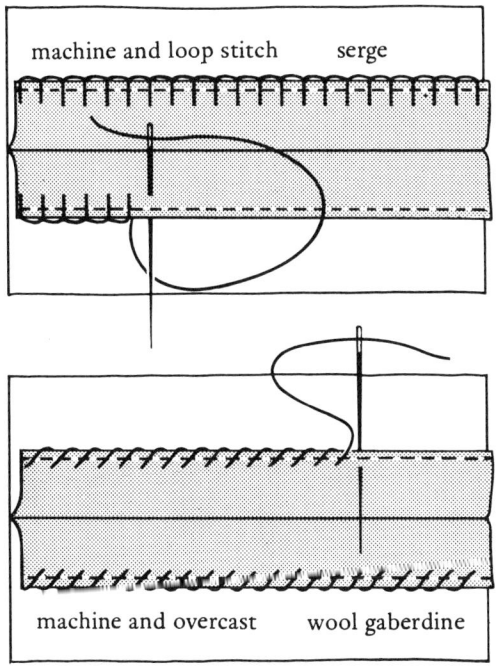

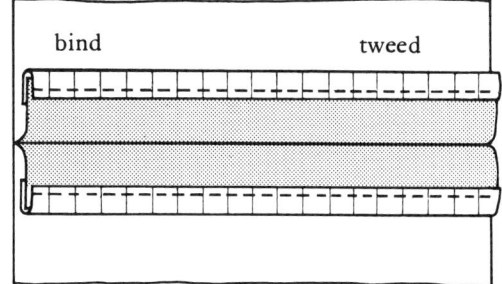

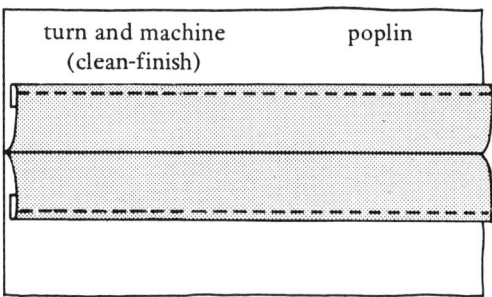

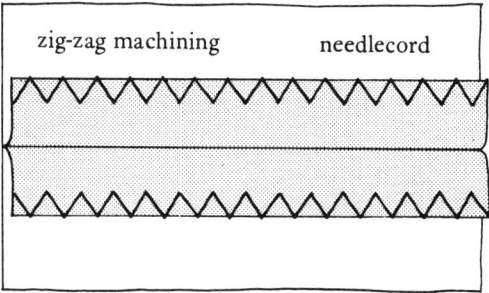

(ii) wool double jersey; does not fray or
ladder (2)
(iii) press seam open, then together (2);
zig-zag 5 mm from F.L. (2), trim carefully,
close to zig-zag stitching (2) *or* machine
again 5 mm from F.L. (2) trim close to
machining (1) zig-zag over machining and
cut edges (1); suitable fabric: e.g. printed
cotton (1); thread type (1), needle size
(1), stitch length (1), stitch width (1), all
to be appropriate to fabric given.

$$\frac{37}{50}$$

Answer 10

a.   (i) 4, (ii) 3, (iii) 2, (iv) 5, (v) 1
b.   (i) 2, (ii) 3, (iii) 5, (iv) 1 (v) 4
c.   (i) 4, (ii), 3 (iii) 5, (iv) 2, (v) 1
d.   (i) 5, (ii) 4, (iii) 1, (iv) 3, (v) 2
e.   (i) 2, (ii) 4, (iii) 5, (iv) 3, (v) 1
f.   (i) 5, (ii) 4, (iii) 1, (iv) 2, (v) 3
g.   (i) 3, (ii) 1, (iii) 5, (iv) 2, (v) 4
h.   (i) 3, (ii) 5, (iii) 2, (iv) 1, (v) 4
i.   (i) 2, (ii) 4, (iii) 5, (iv) 3, (v) 1
j.   (i) 4, (ii) 3, (iii) 5, (iv) 2, (v) 1

(1 mark for each)   50

Answer 11

a. soft, non-irritant, fine, hardwearing, strong, washable, absorbent, non-flammable, opaque (any six, 1 each) 6

b. names of two fabrics (2), descriptions of two fabrics (6) 8

c. curved edge/stretch 2

d. (i) A1 edge of crossway below edge of garment, A2 machining on F.L., A3 W.S. crossway, A4 R.S. garment, A5 seam; B6 R.S. facing, B7 slip hemming, B8 F.L. and machining of seam, B9 W.S. garment, B10 turning on crossway facing, B11 F.L. (1 for each)

(ii) hemming (1), for strength (1)

(iii) roll seam slightly to W.S. (2) 15

e. (i) French (1)

(ii) raw edges enclosed, wears well (2)

(iii) W.S. together, match notches, raw edges together, tack, machine 9 mm from edge, tacks out, trim to 3 mm, R.S. together, tack, machine on fitting line, tacks out (11)

(iv) after trimming, after turning R.S. together (2)

(v) no groove, seam on edge (2)

(vi) back (1) 19

—

50

Answer 12

a. A. trimming scissors: cutting threads, layering turnings, etc. (1 + 2) x 2

B. pinking shears: cutting out linings, felt, neatening samples, etc. 6

b. (i) small wheel (1) inside balance wheel (1); release to wind bobbin (1), stops action of needle (1)

(ii) two rows of teeth (1) raised slightly (1) moves with circular action (1) moves fabric forward for next stitch (1)

(iii) slides or lifts (1) for access to bobbin (1), prevents fabric from entering machine (1)

(iv) two toes (1), needle enters between toes (1); holds fabric in place (1)

(v) arm with hole (1), moves up and down (1) controls quantity of thread for each stitch (1)

(vi) hole for needle (1) and slot for teeth (feed) (1) stops fabric entering machine (1) 20

c. thread from reel in correct position; wound evenly; not too full; same type of thread as on reel to be used; inserted the correct way; thread through the tension spring (1 mark for each) 6

d. easy recognition of size, colour shows when needle inserted, therefore easy to see if correct size is in machine (1)

colours (3), sizes (3): pink 75/11, green 90/14, blue 100/16 7

e. darning: long, wide oval eye, various sizes, thick (4)

beading: long, very fine, small eye, various sizes, thin (4) 8

f. A sharps, B crewel, C betweens 3

—

50

Answer 13

a. button and buttonhole: worked by hand, machine or bound/piped, button and rouleau loop or worked loop, link buttons with two or four holes, frog and Chinese ball button, button over a press stud (5); suitable positions (5)   10

b. closer fit, easier to put on and take off, easier to iron   2

c. (i) 1 machine neatening, 2 tacking — length of opening, 3 raw edges together, 4 R.S. sleeve, 5 W.S. facing, 6 one stitch across base, 7 cut, 8 machining, 9 neatening, 10 edge of opening, 11 W.S. sleeve, 12 R.S. facing (1 mark for each); faced opening (1)

(ii)

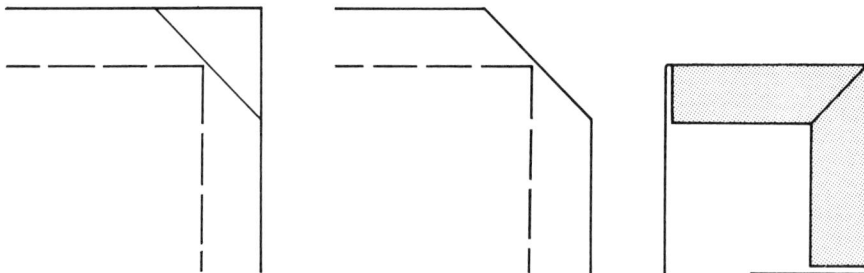

crease F.L. on both adjacent sides (2), crease through corner, edges equal (3), cut off corner (1), mark R.S. and W.S., mitre (edges meet) (3); mitred corner (1)

(iii) 4–6 mm (1)

(iv) machine all round very close to edge of opening (1); loop stitch close together, 1 cm either side of point of opening (1)

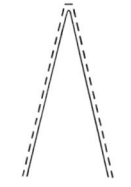 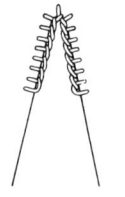

diagrams (2)   28

d. (i) continuous strip (wrap); bound (2)
(ii) bound (1): raw edges together, no shadow (1)   4

e. faced, S.G. 10 x 7 cm; continuous strip, S.G. 18 x 4 cm; bound, crossway 18 x 3 cm (2 x 3)   6
       —
       50

Answer 14

a.   suitable design with small circles suitably
spaced or overlapped to give pleasing design.   4

b.   (i) type of thread (1) three stitches (3)
      colours — to include felt (2)
      (ii) diagrams:-
      needle in (1) needle out (1) thread in relation
      to needle (1) finished stitch (1) (x3)   18

c.   (i) measure circumference of circle — tape
      on edge or piece of string (2)
      (ii) e.g. stab stitch or loop stitch (1)   3

d.   (i) sawdust or bran — firm, prevents rust
      (1 + 2)
      (ii) easy to use, safer, not so many rust,
      pins not lost (4)   7

e.   (i) same size and design, use top and base (3)
      (ii) flannel, felt, vilene. (1) loop stitch or cut
      with pinking shears (1)
      (iii) diagram (4)   9

f.

needle	purpose	sizes
crewel	sewing with wool and embroidery	3/5
sharps	repairs and general work	7/8
darner	darning	5
	(1 + 1 + 1) x 3	9

50

Answer 15

a. *blouse* over-blouse, hip length, faced keyhole neck, bust darts, C.B. zip, long gathered sleeves, bound wrist (7)
skirt four pieces, A-line, side zip (3)   10

b. name (1), description (3), for (i) and (ii)   8

c. good reasons (3 + 3)   6

d. hook and worked bar, button and rouleau loop, button and worked loop etc.   3

e. (i) pattern pieces correctly placed and labelled (5), position of crossway strips indicated (1), economical layout (1)
(ii) back: S.G. ($\frac{1}{2}$), F.L. (1), hem ($\frac{1}{2}$), armhole notches ($\frac{1}{2}$), shoulder notch ($\frac{1}{2}$), length of opening ($\frac{1}{2}$), balance mark ($\frac{1}{2}$)
front: fold ($\frac{1}{2}$), F.L. (1), hem ($\frac{1}{2}$), armhole notch ($\frac{1}{2}$), shoulder notch ($\frac{1}{2}$), dart (1), balance mark ($\frac{1}{2}$)
back facing: S.G. ($\frac{1}{2}$), F.L. ($\frac{1}{2}$), notch ($\frac{1}{2}$)
front facing: fold ($\frac{1}{2}$), F.L. ($\frac{1}{2}$), notch ($\frac{1}{2}$)
sleeve: S.G. ($\frac{1}{2}$), F.L. (1), notches (1), balance marks (1)
(iii) 1.75 metres (1) $\dfrac{23}{50}$

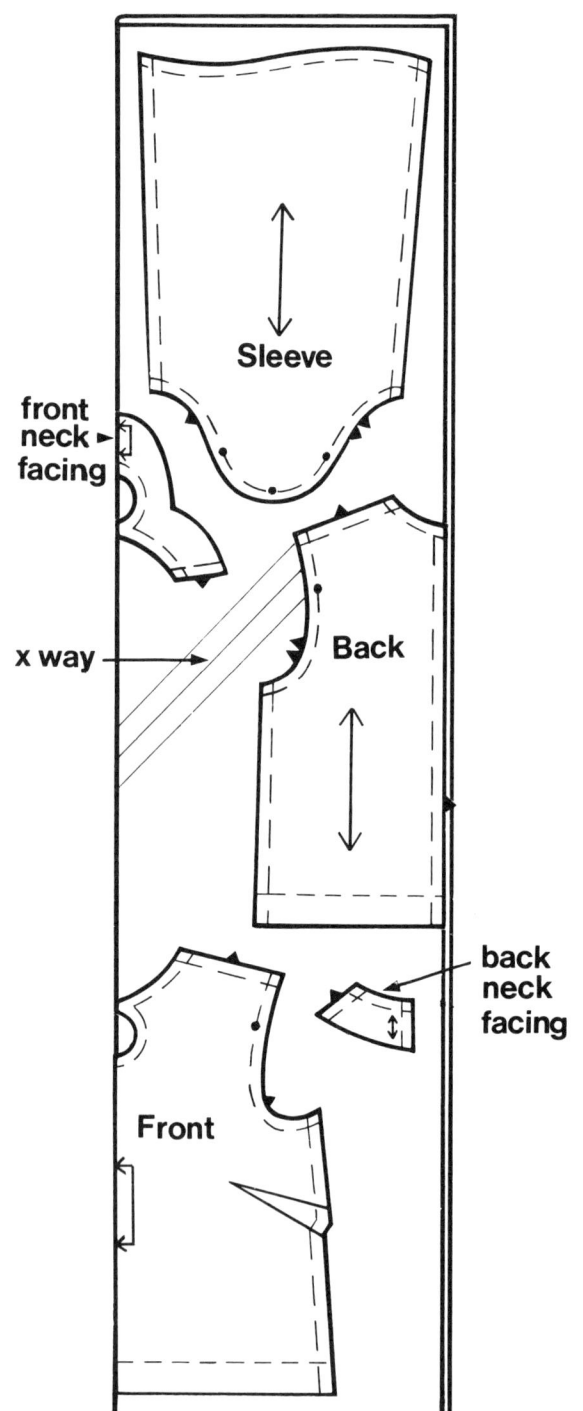

Answer 16

a. (i) 1 machining of zip. 2 S.A., 3 lay (neatened edge) 4 machining, 5 machining on F.L., 6 seams together 7 clip to release, 8 R.S. garment, 9 W.S. facing, 10 one stitch, 11 corner trimmed off, 12 corner of seam trimmed, 13 S.A. turned back, 14 turnings layered, 15 turnings clipped (1 mark for each)

(ii) match seams (1), hem the edge of the facing to the seam (2)   18

b. (i) binding (1)

(ii) 1 work the underarm seam, 2 work gathers, 3 join crossway strip, 4 place R.S. crossway to R.S. sleeve, 5 spread gathers evenly, 6 tack, 7 machine, 8 remove tackings and gathers that show, 9 trim off F.L., 10 turn under raw edge of crossway strip, 11 turn binding to W.S., 12 tack folded edge just above the machining, 13 hem into machine stitching, 14 press (14)   15

c. underarm seams, front notches, back notches, head of sleeve to shoulder seam, balance marks   5

d. e.g. self binding, loop stitch, overcasting, binding   2

e. bra, pants, slip (3); anti-stat, non-irritant, washable, strong, not transparent, good fit, colour suitable (7)   10
                                   ___
                                   50

Answer 17

a. (i) invisible, trouser, closed end, open end (4)

(ii) style, colour, length, weight/type (4)   8

b. (i) A1 tacking on F.L. (2), A2 W.S. fabric (1), A3 notches matching (1), A4 machining on F.L. (2), A5 ends woven back (2), A6 seam allowances (1); B1 S.A. pressed open (2), B2 neatened edge (1), B3 F.L. of garment (1), B4 machining (1); C1 W.S. tape (2), C2 W.S. slide 5 mm below F.L. (3), C3 machining (1), C4 ends of tape loop stitched to S.A. to neaten and secure (3)

(ii) diagram (6)

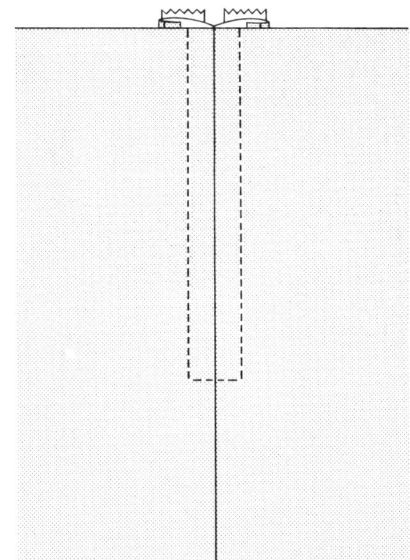

(iii) semi-concealed (1)

(iv) concealed and decorative (visible) (2)

(v) skill, availability of zip foot, width of seam allowance, position, fabric type (5)   37

c. (i) certain fabrics, e g lace and velvet (1); insertion on curved seam (1)

(ii) stab stitch or half back stitch (1); work on R.S. (1); 2 mm − every two teeth (1)   5
                                   ___
                                   50

                                   87

Answer 18

a. C.B. seam $(\frac{1}{2})$, zip — length $(\frac{1}{2})$, two armhole
  seams (1), neckline $(\frac{1}{2})$, collar opening $(\frac{1}{2})$ 3

b. (i) name of fabric (1), description of fabric (3)
  (ii) zip, 1, dress weight, 25 cm (4)
  thread, 1 reel, Sylko, Drima or Trylko, 40 (4)
  buttons, 8, with shanks, 13 mm or 20 line (4)
  elastic, 0.75 m, nylon, 20 mm wide (4)
  hooks and eyes, 2, silver, size 1 (4)   24

c. back trouser, front trouser, C.F. panel, back,
sleeve, collar, side front (7); C.F. panel *underlined,* collar *ticked* (2)   9

d. top stitching, ric-rac, braid, etc.   2

e. 1 first turn 6 mm, 2 R.S., 3 buttonhole for elastic,
4 seams matched, 5 seam allowance, 6 W.S. (1 for
each)   6

f. (i) 2.5 cm (1)
  (ii) for strength, to prevent rolling of elastic,
  for comfort in wear (3)
  (iii) zig-zag machining, 2.5 cm (2)   6
  ___
    50

Answer 19

a. 1. fitted waist, Princess line dress (bust),
  underarm magyar sleeve, crutch on trousers.   4
  2. (i) must be non-fraying and non-rolling (2)
    (ii) finish must be suitable for fabric
    stated (4)   6
  3. (i) seams press flatter, reduces bulk (2)
    (ii) join interfacing pieces together by
    overlapping 3 cm and stitching through
    F.L., trim to stitching on both sides,
    apply to W.S. garment after pressing
    garment seams open (7)   9
  4. (i) neckline, armhole (2)
    (ii) attach facing at seams by hemming (2)
    (iii) layer and clip (2), to reduce bulk and
    allow facing to turn over flat (2)   8
  5. (i) loosen tension (1)
    (ii) two rows (1), 3 mm either side of
    F.L. or on F.L. and 3 mm above (2)
    (iii) W.S. (1)   5
  6. (i) decorative stitching, parallel to edge,
    by machine (2)
    (ii) shiny, twisted, much thicker than
    normal thread (3)
    (iii) more decorative, shows up (1)
    (iv) Drima bold: colour matches with
    sewing thread, all purpose (2)   8
  7. (i) Drima, Trylko, etc. (2)
    (ii) it stretches (1)
    (iii) tricot, jersey wool, double knit Cour-
    telle, etc. (fibres only not acceptable) (3)   6

b. A = R.S., B = W.S., C = interfacing, D = lining   4
  ___
    50

Answer 20

a. repair before a hole appears; work on W.S.;
use yarn of matching colour; use yarn of matching
texture/type; use yarn of matching thickness;
work irregular shape, covering all worn area;
leave loops to allow for shrinkage and stretch;
work warp way; use small stitches; no firm be-
ginning or ending   10

b. work on R.S., horizontally, keep even
tension, work R to L, over a thin place, new
wool is threaded into the knitted stitches to
reinforce it, needle behind upper and lower
loops, alternately   10

c. thin place (1): on knitteds, before a hole
appears (1)
small hole (1): on knitteds for a small hole (1)
hedge tear (1): on wovens, three cornered (1)
cross cut (1): on wovens, bias cut (1)
machined (1): on wovens, towels, house-
hold linen (1)   10

d. fishbone stitch (1); on a cut where there
is no worn area (1); to hold edges together prior
to darning (2); work on W.S. (1), use fine (1)
matching thread (1), fasten on with a few
running stitches (2) from R.H. side of slit (1),
pass needle under one edge (1), then under
other edge (1), drawing (1) edges together (1)   14

e. (i) L-shaped tear (2)

(ii)

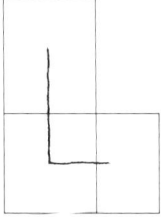

(4) $\dfrac{6}{50}$

Answer 21

a. A reversible, without nap (2); B one way, with
nap (2); C uneven check — one way, with nap (2)   6

b. A (2), B (2), C (2)   6

c. (i) add 1.5 cm at C.F., add notch, extend
neck and waist edges (4); draw S.G. arrow
45° to fold arrow (2)
(ii) single fabric, cut twice, S.G. arrow,
checks match reverse pattern (5)   11

d. (i) slip tacking (1), 1 R.S. (1), 2 vertical pins (1),
3 needle through single fabric (2), 4 stripes matching (1), 5 F.L. together (1), 6 seam allowances
together (1)
(ii) smaller tacking (1); pin (1) across F.L. (1)
at every matching stripe (1) and machine
over pins (1)   13

e. (i) bodice front, pocket (2)
(ii) bodice: stay stitch and interface C.F. (2)
pocket: line with fabric on S.G. (1)
(iii) attaching collar, facing, 3 cm (1 + 1 + 1);
sleeve edge, binding, 5 cm (1 + 1 + 1); between
bodice and skirt, piping, 4 cm (1 + 1 + 1)   14
                                                                            $\overline{50}$

Answer 22

a.

front view showing scoop neck, gathers under
bust, seam under bust, waist seam, cuff, gathers
into cuff, armhole seams, no fullness at sleeve
head, bias cut skirt (9)

back view showing armhole seams, no fullness at
sleeve head, neckline, C.B. zip, length of zip,
C.B. seam, waist seam, midriff seam, bodice
darts, shoulder darts, cuff opening, cuff, fullness
into cuff (13)   22

b.   name of fabric (1), description (3),
reasons (3)   7

c.   thread, 2 reels, type, size (4)
    zip, 1, type, length (3)
    buttons, 2, type, size (4)   11

d.   (i) neck, midriff, cuff (3)
    (ii) type (1), length and width (2)   6

e.   type (1), reasons relating to fabric in (*b*) (2),
size in relation to button given in (*c*) (1)   4
                                                              ———
                                                               50

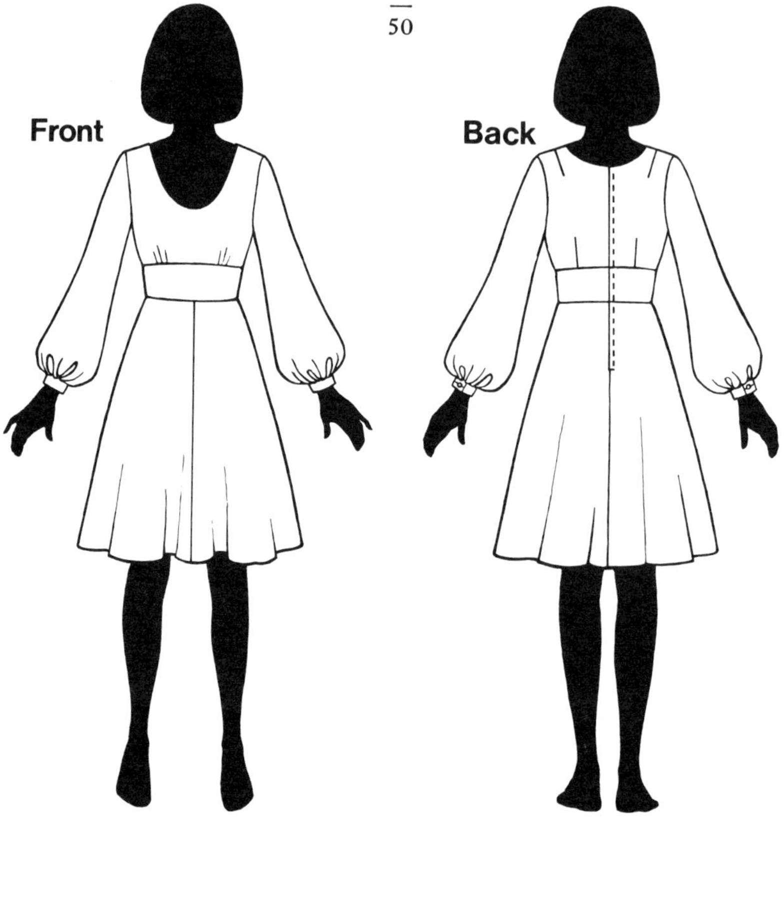

Front   **Back**

Answer 23

a. (i) two rows, in correct position for figure, small, even stitches (4)

(ii) darts to C.B., side seams matched, both sides of C.B. midriff of equal depth, smooth line of stitching to skirt and to bodice (5)

(iii) top of slide 5 mm below F.L. at neck, good midriff cross joins, firm tacking, machine same direction both sides, edges of fabric meeting to conceal zip (5)

(iv) good shape, layer turnings, clip turnings, understitch, attach facing to seams (5)

(v) sleeves into correct armholes with balance marks and notches matched, easing threads pulled up carefully so that no gathers or pleats are formed, smooth underarm, underarm seams matching, good fit on shoulder (5)

(vi) made up correctly for L and R sleeve, correct wrap, matching balance marks and notches, correct depth all round especially at ends, strong hand stitching (5)

(vii) allow to drop (by hanging) wear garment with correct shoes, all fasteners done up, measure from floor up, keep very still while hem is measured (5)   34

b. iron, sleeve board, ham, cloth, ironing board (5)
cuffs, sleeves, midriff, bodice, neckline, skirt (5)   10

c. three sketches showing interesting ideas
                     (2 x 3)   6
                                        50

Answer 24

a. empty pockets, remove fluff, remove or secure buttons, repair if necessary or list repairs to be done at cleaners, remove badges, mark stains for special treatment   5

b. treat as soon as possible, kind of stain, type of fabric, agent to use (try mildest first), test on W.S.   5

c. milk: ink; salt: blood, egg (protein); methylated spirit: grass, biro; glycerine: lipstick, tea, coffee, vegetable stains; lemon juice: (+ salt) iron mould, some biro   5

d. rest between wear, air after wear, hang after wear, use correct size of hanger, brush well, remove marks, repair as necessary, attach skirt loops at C.F. and C.B. as well as at sides.   8

e. wash daily, use mild detergent, wash by hand, rinse well, squeeze out excess water in towel, dry away from direct heat   4

f. (i) work a bar tack, (ii) place tape on W.S., (iii) work an arrow head, (iv) neaten by overcasting or loop stitch, (v) another row of stitching and neatening   5

g. (i) diagrams (3)

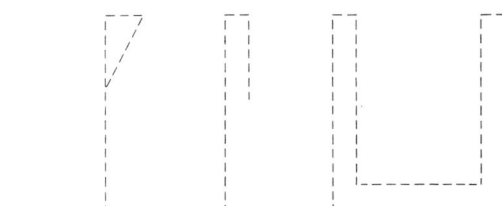

(ii) cut 3 cm squares of tailor's canvas, neaten edges by overcasting, tack to wrong side at points of stress, stitch through garment and canvas (5)   8

h 1 W.S. garment (1), 2 seam neatened (1), 3 seam allowance clipped (1), 4 clips neatened with loop stitch (1), 5 F.L. of under-arm seam — seam pressed open (2), 6 bias strip (1), 7 3 mm turned to W.S. (1), 8 machining very close to edge, through to R.S. (2) 10
                                        50

Answer 25

a. names (1 for each), descriptions of two
fabrics (3 for each), 5 good reasons for choice (5) 13
b. 1 bound neckline (1), 2 bound armholes (1), 3
decorative buttons (1), 4 straight yoke (1), 5 crossway
flaps (1), 6 knife pleated skirt (2)   7
c. thread; quantity, type and size depend on
    fabric chosen (4)
    binding, 1 card, bias binding, colour to
    tone (4)
    buttons, 3, with shank, 15 mm diameter (4)
    zip, 1, nylon teeth, approximately 30 cm (4)
    hook and eye, 1, silver, size 0 (4)   20
d. (i) exactly on the cross, cut matching pair (2)
    (ii) 1 W.S. (1), 2 machining on F.L. (2), 3 turn-
    ings layered (1), 4 notched curve (1), 5 R.S. (1),
    6 edge tacking (1), 7 seam rolled underneath (1)
                                                      10
                                                    ――
                                                      50

Answer 26

a. 1 interface (1): to add body, to keep shape (1)
    2 machine on F.L. (1): to give correct size
    of cuff when completed (1)
    3 interfacing cut down to machining (1):
    to reduce bulk of turnings (1)
    4 clip for wrap (1): to ease application to
    sleeve and to form wrap (1)
    5 layer turnings (seam allowance) (1):
    to eliminate hard line when pressed (1)
    6 cut off corner (1): to give square
    corners on cuff (1)   12

b. *Sew invisibly*: pick up one thread (1), use
matching thread to fabric (1), take care that
stitches do not show on R.S. (1)
Pull threads to adjust fullness: gathering
threads (1), arrange fullness evenly (1),
check effect on R.S. (1)
Stitch: machine (1) on F.L. (1)
Trim: trim interfacing to machining (2),
layer (1) gathered edge (1), cut off notches (1)
Stitch ends: machine on F.L. (1) level with
opening edge (1), right angle to other
stitching (1)
Trim: trim interfacing to machining (1),
layer turnings (1), cut off corners (1)
Slip stitch remaining edge over seam: turn
S.A. of free edge of cuff to W.S. (1), tack
and slip hem to the machining (1), stitching
must not show on R.S. (1)
Top stitch: machine on R.S. (1) for decoration (1) using larger machine stitch (1),
thread may be thicker or of contrasting
colour (1)
Pivoting: needle in fabric at corner (1),
lift foot (1), turn cuff (1), check angle (1),
lower foot (1), continue machining (1)   32
c. (i) sensible reasons for method preferred (2)
    (ii) correct position of button and buttonhole (2)

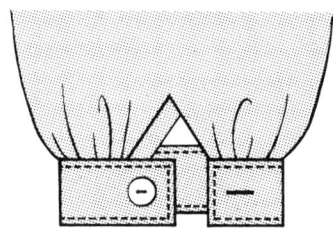

(iii) correct markings (2)

                                                       6
                                                      ――
                                                      50

Answer 27

a. (i) mitre tape above slide (1), open out tapes
to be at right angles with zip (2), level with
top fitting line (1), back stitch the dart so
formed (2), do not clip off ends of tape (2)
(ii) inserting an open ended zip without a
facing and C.B. when zip is applied after
lining (2)
(iii) end of zip tape should be neatened with
loop stitch (2) to lengthen wear, prevent
fray and anchor tape (3)   15

b. (i) lingerie loop — shoulder strap loop (1)
(ii) on sleeveless garments with narrow
shoulders (1) to prevent shoulder straps
slipping off shoulders (2)
(iii) use either 5 mm wide ribbon, tape or
rouleau (1), cut length of approximately
5 cm (1), turn under one end 5 mm (2),
place centrally on seam allowance at shoulder
(2), attach three sides (1) by hemming (1)
and fourth (1) by back stitch (1), sew tiny
press stud to fitting line of shoulder (2),
other section to be sewn to neatened free
edge of ribbon so that it is flat when
fastened (4)   20

c. (i) mitre (1)
(ii) patch pocket (1)
(iii) crease F.L. on side and base (2), turn
in point until it meets F.L. of corner (2),
trim off leaving 5 mm (2), turn in and
press side and base on F.L.s (3), tack in
position, edges should meet (2)
(iv) the raw edges should be turned under
and tacked (2)   15
                                             ––
                                             50

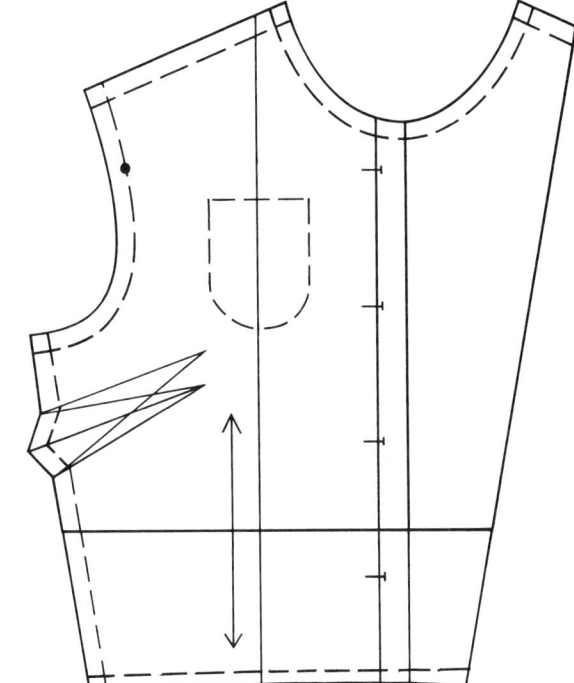

(i) 1 facing, 2 fold line, 3 C.F. (3)
(ii) Buttonholes 4   = 1
    Equally spaced   = 3
    At 90° to C.F.   = 1
    Extend beyond C.F. = 1   (6)
(iii) Dart raise point   = 1
    directly above   = 1
    join to original line = 2   (4)
(iv) position of fitting line (4), seam
allowance 1.5 cm (1)
(v) (see diagram) (2)
(vi) pocket marking (2)
(vii) e.g. balance mark and S.G. line (2 x 2)   26

c. A1 W.S. facing, A2 machine on F.L., A3 neatening of facing by folding 3 mm to W.S., A4 R.S. pocket,
A5 F.L., A6 notch to remove bulk, A7 machining,
A8 layer to reduce bulk, A9 corners off to reduce
bulk (9); B1 R.S. facing, B2 free edge of facing
neatened, B3 notches closed, B4 S.A., B5 F.L.,
B6 W.S. pocket (6); C1 triangle of machining to
lengthen, C2 machining close to pocket edge, C3
long and short tacking (3)   18
                                              ––
                                              50

Answer 28

a. study the pattern and instructions, check
the pattern measurements, adjust the pattern,
prepare the fabric, plan the layout, pin   6

Answer 29

a. 1 straight shoulder yoke (2), 2 short puff sleeve (2), 3 pointed shirt collar (2), 4 button and button-hole fastening (2), 5 square patch pocket (2) 10

b. front, front yoke, back, back yoke, pocket, sleeve, cuff, collar, back neck facing (1 for each) 9

c. collar, cuff, centre front (1 for each) 3

d. accept sketches if given and any suitable combination of mix and match fabrics, e.g. pocket, collar, cuff and yoke; collar, yoke, sleeve and cuff; collar, cuff and pocket 4

e. A. apply interfacing to cuff, pin sleeve to cuff on F.L., match balance marks, adjust gathers, tack, machine on F.L, trim gathers, remove tacking, layer interfacing, press seam to band, turn free edge to W.S. on F.L., press (12)
B. join the underarm seam, R.S. together, match notches, pin and tack, machine on F.L., trim interfacing to stitches (6)
C. press seam open, turn band to W.S. on fold line, tack, hem into machine stitches, remove tacking, press (6) 24
—
50

Answer 30

a. (i)

(ii) hand or machine wash, medium wash (by machine), water at 50°C (hand hot), cold rinse, short spin or drip dry (5); do not use bleach (1); iron temperature, warm (150°C) (2); dry clean with perchlorethylene or white spirit only (3) 18

b. 1 Woolmark: pure new wool (all virgin wool, 100 per cent new wool) (2)
2 polyester fibre (1)
3 anti-static finish, treated to prevent the build up of static electricity, does not attract dirt, garment stays clean longer, stops 'riding up' (5)
4 'Blue C' nylon fabric made by Monsanto, guaranteed for one year from date of purchase if subjected to normal wear (4)
5 leather (1)
6 Koratron: treated garment, pressed and shaped for ever which can be machine washed and does not need ironing (3)
7 nylon made by Courtaulds (2) 18

c. (i) machine washable, warm medium wash 40°C, rinse at same temperature, spin or machine wring, dry cloth, warm iron (7)

(ii) machine or hand wash 48°C, cold rinse, short spin or drip dry, cool iron if required, setting 1 (100°C) (7) 14
—
50

Answer 31

a. 1 yoke cut on cross (2), 2 button and buttonhole fastening (2), 3 gathers above bustline (2), 4 continuous wrap opening (2), 5 puffed sleeve (2), 6 top stitched yoke (2), 7 fitted sleeve band (2) 14

b. (i) synthetic, coal, air, water (4)
(ii) soft, gathers well, hardwearing, drip dry, easy care (4) 8

c. (i) natural, America, Africa, India (4)
(ii) check (1)
(iii) dying, printing (2) 7

d. name (1) description (3) x 2 8

e. (i) plain, weft, warp (3)
(ii) twill, satin, etc. (2) 5

f. 1 sleeve band, 2 sleeve, 3 yoke W.S., 4 yoke R.S., 5 opening W.S., 6 opening R.S., 7 skirt seams and hem W.S., skirt R.S. 8

—
50

Answer 32

a. (i) 1 front skirt, 2 back skirt, 3 back yoke, 4 front yoke, 5 sleeve (1 for each)
(ii) sleeve band (cuff) (1) 6

b. (i) economical layout (1)
(ii) front skirt and back skirt: to fold (2), back yoke: to fold, twice (2), front yoke: on correct grain, twice (2), sleeve: straight grain (1), band: size and shape (1), straight grain (1)
(iii) measure layout x 10 (scale 1 : 10), answer in cm, convert to metres (3)
(iv) thread, buttons, press studs, thread for top stitching, interfacing (3) 16

c. 1 W.S. yoke, 2 shoulder seam pressed open, 3 machining on F.L., 4 turnings layered, 5 turnings clipped, 6 corner trimmed off, 7 C.F. marked by tacking, 8 edge tacking at neckline, 9 both layers pinned together, 10 basted flat on R.S., 11 S.A. turned to W.S., 12 both layers tacked together, seams matching, (1 mark for each) 12

d. 1 W.S. yoke, 2 S.A. turned to W.S. and tacked, 3 gathering threads, 4 gathering threads pulled up and secured around a pin, 5 R.S. yoke, 6 vertical pins, 7 fitting lines matching, 8 R.S. skirt (1 mark for each) 8

e. running stitch: gathers (2)
buttonhole stitch: buttonholes and press studs (2)
hemming: opening, yoke and sleeve band (2)
slip hemming: hem (2) 8

—
50

Answer 33

a. (i) 1   mercerized, shiny, twisted, different
thicknesses (3)
    2   mercerized, five thick, eight thin,
marked twist (3)
    3   dull, quite thick, twisted (3)
    4   mercerized cotton, six strands, used
together or separately (3)
    5   dull, very thick, loosely twisted (3)
    6   mercerized, very thick, loosely twisted (3)
    7   dull, quite thick, twisted, soft (3)

(ii) e.g.

	embroidery	*fabric*
1	blackwork (1)	evenweave linen (1)
2	hardanger (1)	double thread linen (1)
3	cross stitch (1)	binca (1)
4	smocking (1)	gingham (1)
5	needleweaving (1)	crash (1)
6	couching (1)	hessian (1)
7	tent stitch (1)	canvas (1)

(iii)

	needle type	*needle size*
1	tapestry ($\frac{1}{2}$)	7/8 ($\frac{1}{2}$)
2	tapestry ($\frac{1}{2}$)	5/7 ($\frac{1}{2}$)
3	tapestry ($\frac{1}{2}$)	22 ($\frac{1}{2}$)
4	crewel ($\frac{1}{2}$)	7 ($\frac{1}{2}$)
5	chenille ($\frac{1}{2}$)	11 ($\frac{1}{2}$)
6	chenille ($\frac{1}{2}$)	11 ($\frac{1}{2}$)
7	tapestry ($\frac{1}{2}$)	5 ($\frac{1}{2}$) 42

b. change foot (1), thread top and bobbin with
machine embroidery thread (2), adjust tension
according to machine instructions (1), needle size
60–70 (1), set stitch selector, stitch width and
stitch length to correct position for stitch
required (2), test on spare fabric (1)   8
                                         —
                                       50

Answer 34

a. 1 seam neatened and pressed open (2), 2 hem
length marked and turned up on line of tacking (3),
3 seams matching (1), 4 tacked close to fold (2), 5
narrow lay turned to W.S. (2), 6 pinned vertically
(2), 7 fullness arranged evenly in darts (2), 8 darts
tacked in position (1), 9 W.S. (1), 10 hem tacked to
garment (2), 11 darts hemmed in position (1), 12 hem
slip-hemmed to garment (2), 13 hemming used at
seams for strength (3), 14 finished hem (1)   25

b. (i) cotton poplin, cotton satin, etc. (2)
no more than 10 cm (1)
(ii) Sylko: 40, sharps: 8 (4)

(iii) W.S., , folded edge only, dry
heat (4)   11

c. (i) gathers used instead of darts (2), no
turning at upper edge (2), bias strip applied
to raw edge as a facing (2); less bulky on
thicker fabrics (2)

(ii) probably cooler iron (1) steam
pressing instead of dry pressing (2)   11

d. (i) straight skirt hem on thick fabric (2)
(ii) e.g. scallops, false hem (1)   3
                                         —
                                     50

Answer 35

a. (i) straight, waist, ease, 15, seam allowance, two, width, two, 1 cm (9)

(ii) petersham, buckram, iron-on Vilene, Staflex, etc. (3)

(iii) 1 stiffening basted into place, 2 seam allowance tacked in position, 3 W.S. fabric, 4 fitting line marked, 5 slightly narrower section, 6 snip, 7 fold in neatly, 8 catch stitch raw edge to stiffening, 9 seam allowance turned to W.S., 10 pin vertically (1 mark for each) 11 slip hem (1)

(iv) 1 R.S., 2 W.S., 3 seam just to W.S., 4 eyelets, 5 hemming to secure buckle, 6 carrier to support end of fastened belt, 7 eyelet for buckle prong (1 mark for each)   30

b. (i) A   mark position (1) and size (1), work running stitches (1) round mark;
B   pierce (1) with stiletto (1), work through all layers (1) to open hole (1);
C   overcast finely (1) to neaten (1), pull taut (1) to keep hole open (1)

(ii) stronger hole but smaller hole (2)   13

c. (i) ribbon, cord, tape, rouleau, etc. (3)

(ii) sleeve wrist, C.F. neck, outside ankle of trousers (2)

(iii) edge to edge faced (double fabric) (2)   7
                                      50

Answer 36

a. A. (i) plain weave (1)

(ii) weft (1) threads pass alternately (1) under (1) and over (1) single (1) warp (1) threads

(iii) e.g. calico, muslin, cambric, pongee, afgalaine (1)

B. (i) twill (1)

(ii) 2 x 2 twill – the weft threads run over two and under two but in each line they move along one and the finished effect is a series of diagonal lines (6)

(iii) e.g. serge, tartan, denim, drill, foulard, gaberdine (1)

C. (i) satin (1)

(ii) warp floats of five to eight threads; gives a lustrous fabric on R.S. – weft thread passed over one warp then under five (different position on next row) (6)

(iii) e.g. ciré, satin ribbon, tricel satin, bridal and duchesse satin (1)

D. (i) basket weave (1)

(ii) two threads are raised and lowered alternately, two weft threads are woven together (6)

(iii) hopsack (1)   32

b. straight grain: warp/weft straight, parallel to selvedge (2)
selvedge: finished edge, weft wrapped round warp (3)
true cross: $45°$ to warp/weft (2)
bias: $60°/30°$, not so stretchy (2)

diagram (1 mark each of above + 1 mark base fabric)   14

c. needlecord, corduroy, velvet, velveteen   4
                                      50

Answer 37

a.   magyar or kimono   1

b.   shape (6)

                                                        marks/labels (8)

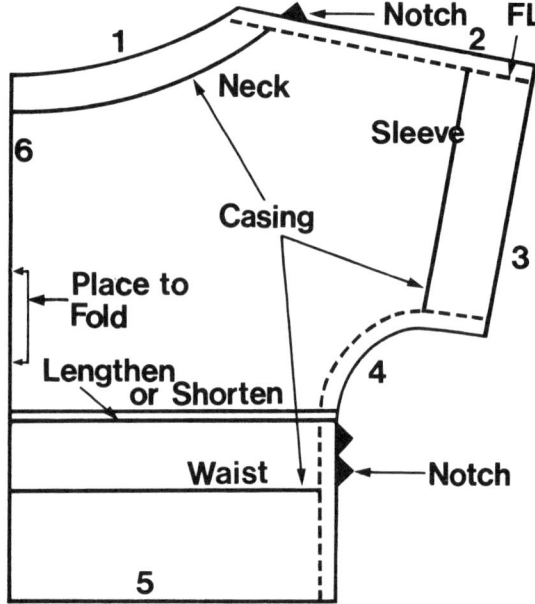

                                                                          14

c.   neck: casing and drawstring (ribbon), sleeve:

       casing and elastic, waist: shirring (1 for each)   3

d.   fabric type (1), description (3), reasons (4)   8

e.   if as above:

       thread, 1 reel, suitable for fabric, size or

       colour

       shirring elastic, 1 spool, fine, colour

       elastic, 0.75 m, white nylon, 5 mm wide

       bias binding, 1 card, nainsook, colour

       ribbon, 1.5 m, nylon, 5 mm wide and

       colour

       thread (tassels), 1 skein, embroidery,

       colour   (1 + 3) x 6   24

                                                                   ——

                                                                   50

Answer 38

a.   (i) 25 cm (1)

       (ii) 10 cm above the waist, 15 cm below

       the waist (2)   3

b.   A.   on W.S. (1) press darts to centre (1),

join waist seam (1), clip off end of waist seam

to reduce bulk (1), neaten (1), press up (1),

join side seam as far as zip (1) and neaten through-

out (1), tack seam on F.L. the length of the zip

opening (1)

       B.   press side seam open (1), centre the

zip (1) face down (1) in position (1), tack both

sides (1), machine zip in place using zip (cording)

foot (2), equal number of stitches at top and

base (2), finish ends on W.S. (1), remove tack-

ings (1)

       C.   bar tack top and base on R.S. (2) for

strength (1), remove tacks in seam (1)   24

c.   (i) wrap and faced placket (2)

       (ii) hook and bar at waistline, press studs

       above and below waist (2)

       (iii) 1. W.S. front of garment, 2. W.S. back of

       garment, 3. S.A., 4. edge neatened by machine,

       5. F.L.s of opening, 6. waistline seam, 7. R.S. of

       facing, 8. R.S. of wrap, 9. pins at right angles, 10.

       fold tacked in position (1 mark for each)

       (iv) open seam and turnings must be en-

       closed in wrap (2)

       (v) hemming (1)

       (vi) to reduce bulk (1)

       (vii) the whole seam is clipped, neatened

       and pressed to back, S.A. reduced, width of

       seam wrap and facing pieces to be equal to

       fell of seam when completed (5)   23

                                                                   ——

                                                                   50

Answer 39

a.

	collar	neckline	garment
A	sailor	I	tunic
B	mandarin	G	housecoat
C	crossway roll	F	dress
D	shirt	J	jacket
E	tie	H	blouse
	(5)	(5)	(5)

15

b.   H, I and J (3); all low necklines, therefore neck appears longer (2)   5

c.   any five from: S.G., cut 4, notch, balance mark, fitting line, piece number, pattern number, make (mark (1) label (1) x 5)   10

d.   1. machining on F.L., 2. notches matching, 3. fitting line of neck, 4. turnings layered (graded or trimmed), 5. notched seam allowance, 6. interfacing cut to machine stitches,   6

e.   1. turn to R.S. (1), 2. roll edge tack seam (2),
      3. tack neck edges together on fitting line (2),
4. press well (1)   6

f.   (i) shaped facing, crossway facing, lined yoke (3)
      (ii) lined yoke (1): firmer, neater, warmer, harder wearing (4)   8
                                                                                ──
                                                                                50

Answer 40

a.   (i) s̲k̲i̲r̲t̲ ̲f̲r̲o̲n̲t̲, s̲k̲i̲r̲t̲ ̲b̲a̲c̲k̲, strap, bib, bib lining, waistband (6)
      (ii) underlined as above (2)
      (iii) waistband (1)   9

b.   diagram showing at least two tucks   6

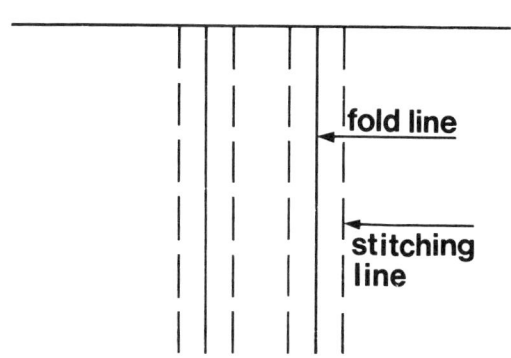

c.   (i) unpressed (1) pleats (1)
      (ii) diagram (10)

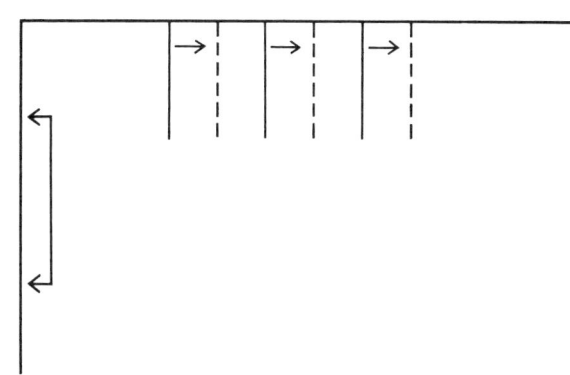

      (iii) darts, smocking, easing, shirring, gauging — any 4 (4)   16

d.   1. machining on F.L. (2), 2. waistband trimmed (2), 3. bib layered (2), 4. waistband (1), 5. interfacing (1), 6. interfacing tacked on (2), 7. interfacing trimmed to machining (2), 8. corners cut off (2)   14

e.   turn to R.S. (1), work the corners out (1), roll edge (1), edge tack (1), press (1)   5
                                                                                ──
                                                                                50

Answer 41

a.　(i) A. inverted, B. knife, C. box, D. accordian
　　(1 mark for each)
　　(ii) D accordian (1)　　　　　　　　　5
b.　(i) type of fabric (1), fabric weight (1),
　　crease shedding properties (1), heat setting
　　properties for pressing pleats (1)
　　(ii) e.g. A. cotton denim, B. Acrilan tartan, C.
　　woollen tweed, D. tricel foulard (4)
c.　(i) arrow head (1)　　　　　　　　　8
　　(ii) diagram (4)

　　(iii) Drima bold or buttonhole twist (1),
　　crewel size 6 (1)　　　　　　　　　7
d.　edge stitch (1) 2 mm from edge on R.S. (1),
double fabric (1), regular machine stitch (1),
very straight (1), matching thread (1), repeat
on W.S. (1)　　　　　　　　　　　　7
e.

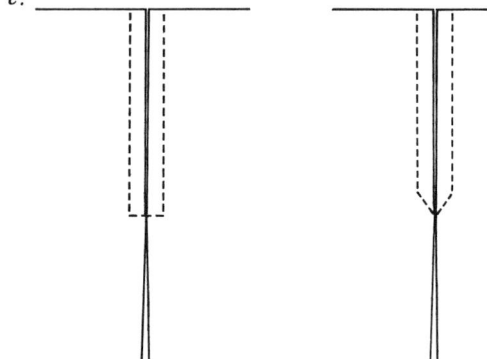

　　(2 marks for each diagram)　　　　　4

f.　pleat up in hand, place in nylon stocking
and hang up　　　　　　　　　　　　3
g.　(i) shape (2)
　　labelled pattern markings (6)

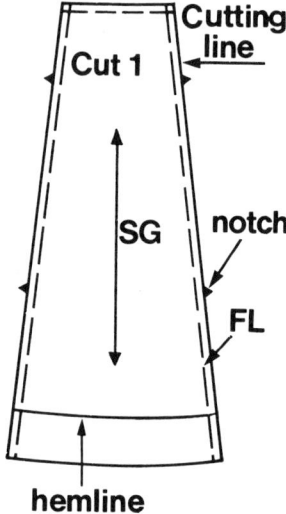

(ii) hem of skirt and inlay completed separately (2), hem lines finished with herringbone (2), final section of seam joined (1),
ends woven in (1), hem is less bulky, pleat
holds in better (2)　　　　　　　　　16
　　　　　　　　　　　　　　　　　──
　　　　　　　　　　　　　　　　　50

Answer 42

a. weft knitting (2): wale, course, loop, continuous yarn with needles (4) 6

b. tights, socks, vests, pants, slips, jumpers, etc. 5

c. wool, cotton, Acrilan, nylon, Terylene, rayon, etc. 6

d. wool jersey (single jersey), stockinette, Crimplene jersey, nylon tricot, brushed nylon, double jersey 5

e. no fraying, easy to handle, crease shedding, often cheaper, quicker to make up, will ease/stretch well 5

f. thread type (1); stretch (1)
needle size (preferably ball point) (1); no hole (1)
stitch size (to include length and swing) (2); stretch (1) 7

g. type of yarn (1), details of laundering (4), care label (3) x 2 16
—
50

Answer 43

a. *jacket*; patch pockets, raglan sleeves, shoulder darts, edge to edge (no fastening), hip length, long sleeves, bust darts (underarm), top stitched, V-neck (9)
   pinafore dress; sleeveless, V neck, top stitched, no darts, C.B. zip, knee length, flared skirt, belted (6) 15

b. *main pieces*; jacket front, jacket back, sleeve, pinafore dress front, pinafore dress back (5)
other pieces for jacket; back neck facing, front facing (2)
other pieces for pinafore dress; front neck facing, back neck facing, front armhole facing, back armhole facing (4) 11

c. 'Use unbonded knits'; use a knitted fabric which is stretchable; no darts in pinafore dress, so stretch is necessary (2)
'Bias printed fabric'; bias design printed on fabric to give effect of bias fabric; necessary to know so that bias cutting is not necessary, fabric allowance given for pattern to be placed on straight grain of fabric (2) 4

d. names of yarns (2), one underlined and five good reasons (6) 8

e. (i) 1. R.S. together, notches matched, raw edges together (3)
   2. stay tape placed centrally on top of fitting line (2)
   3. machine on fitting line through all thicknesses (1)
   (ii) necessary to prevent stretch in wear (1)
   (iii) temperature of iron, press on W.S., use sleeve board, use pressing cloth, press seam open (all with reference to d) (5) 12
—
50

Answer 44

a. names (1 x 2), descriptions (3 x 2)   8
b. four sensible qualities   4
c. seams suitable for fabrics chosen (1 x 2), reasons (3 x 2)   8
d. methods suitable for garments and fabrics   2
e. (i) A1 design of lace overlapped on R.S. (1), A2 running stitches round design (1) A3. over-stitch round design (1) B1. W.S. lace (1), B2. narrow hem on sleeve edge (2), B3. slip-hemming securing hem and lace (2), B4. long and short tacking (1), B5. crossway casing or bias binding casing (2), B6. two rows of machining close to edge (2)

(ii) satin stitch; Drima or similar thread suitable for type of lace selected (2)

(iii) cut off excess carefully both R.S. and W.S., gather lace (4)   19

f. hand wash (1), mild detergent (1), hand hot water − 48°C (1), do not wring (1), rinse well (1), roll in towel to remove excess water (2), cool iron − 100°C (1), on W.S. (1)   9

    —
    50

Answer 45

a.	Nylon	not a family name
b.	Chemical	not a fibre type
c.	North Down	not a breed of sheep
d.	Nylon	not an acrylic fibre
e.	Celon	not a rayon
f.	Rayon	not a natural fibre
g.	Tricel	not a modified fibre
h.	Rayon	not a synthetic fibre
i.	Tricel	not a polyester
j.	Cotton	not a bast fibre
k.	Orlon	not made from a polyamide fibre
l.	Staple fibre	not long
m.	Reeling	not concerned with manufacture of woollen fabric
n.	Retting	not concerned with manufacture of cotton fabric
o.	Sliver	does not occur in manufacture of fibre
p.	Lawn	not made from silk
q.	Tricot	not a weave
r.	Tweed	not a knitted fabric
s.	Satin	not a pile fabric
t.	Worsted	not a mixture
u.	Shantung	not made from wool
v.	Vat	not printing
w.	Brushed	not a lustre finish
x.	Mitin	not a shrink proof finish
y.	Dyed	one colour (1 + 1) x 25 50

Answer 46

a. 1. shoulder yoke, 2. armhole ruffle, 3. sweetheart neckline, 4. elasticated waist (midriff), 5. hemline frill (5)

Back view (5)   10

b. (i) plain, engraved, rollers, colour, two, scrape, other, fluff, roller, tank (10)
(ii) direct, resist, discharge, duplex, etc. (4)
(iii) same rollers used, but four different sets of colours (2) reds, greens, yellow/browns, blues, etc. (4)   20

c. evenweave, loose, rough effect, R.S. and W.S. alike   4

d. gathering, shirring (elasticating)   2

e. (i) trace tack from pattern (2)
(ii) use machine foot or quilting attachment for guide (2)   4

f. 1. raw edges together, 2. match notches, 3. vertical pins, 4. tack on F.L., 5. W.S. frill, 6 two rows of machine gathers, 7. frill trimmed down 8, machine on F.L., 9. turn in edge of skirt 3 mm, 10. secure binding by hemming into machine stitches   10
             —
             50

Answer 47

a. (i) <u>yoke back</u>, yoke front, armhole frill, hem frill, <u>back</u>, <u>front</u>, <u>back neck facing</u>, <u>front neck facing</u> (8)
(ii) see (i) above (5)   13

b. neck wide enough for head, elasticated midriff allows shoulders through   2

c. tailor tacks; from pattern to fabric; mark matching points
tacking; all pieces together; prior to fitting
gathering; section into front yoke; small section
hemming; self binding of frill; strong for laundering
slip-hemming; hem of frill; inconspicuous (or other suitable stitches with reasons, etc.)   15

d. side, press, cool, shirring, tightly, bobbin, Trylko or Drima, long, test , single, same, right, side seam, long, parallel, evenly, tacks, elastic, securely   20
             —
             50

Answer 48

a. (i) even weave, printed — therefore R.S. darker colours than W.S., smooth, etc. (3)

(ii) interfacing, 0.25 m, organdie thread, 2 reels, Trylko or Drima shirring elastic, 1 reel, white (9)

(iii) size of stitch: 12 per inch (or number 2 setting) size of machine needle: 11 (or 80) (2)

(iv) sharps 9 (2)   16

b. (i) join R.S. together, match notches at shoulder seams, tack, machine on F.L., trim, press open; turn 3 mm to W.S. to neaten free edge, machine close to fold, trim turnings, press (11)

(ii) 1. layer or trim turnings, clip into curve every 2 cm (2)

2. layer or trim turnings, notch every 1.5 cm (2)

3. cut right into corner to ease turning through (2)

(iii) to ease cutting and turning through, good shape on R.S. when turned (3)   20

c. bind with bias binding; machine, trim and loop stitch; machine, trim and overcast; zig-zag and trim (4)

seam should be pressed upwards (1)   5

d. (i) narrow hem to W.S. and slip hem (3)

(ii) narrow hem to W.S. and machine (3)

(iii) single turn to W.S., embroidery stitch on R.S., trim close to machining on W.S. (3)   9
    —
    50

Answer 49

a. tailor tacks (1)

1. facing turned back, 2. fold line, 3. C.F. line, 4. at least half diameter of button, 5. diameter of button + 3 mm 6. R.S. garment (1 mark for each)   7

b. (i) 4.5 to 5.0 cm x 5.0 cm (2)

(ii) crossway or straight grain (1)   3

c. 1. open out garment facing (1) after snipping tailor tacks (1), fold strip in half (1) R.S. out (1), place centrally over marked position (1)

2. open out strip (1), tack in place R.S. together (1), check W.S. position of tacking (1)

3. machine (1) 3 mm away from buttonhole tack on each long side (1), machine exactly across each end (1) with equal number of machine stitches (1), begin machining at centre of a long side (1), overlapping 5 mm to finish (1), cut off ends (1).

4. remove tacks (1), cut through both layers (1) to within 3 mm of each end (1), snip diagonally into each corner (1)

5. turn binding strip to W.S. garment (1), work ends to good oblong shape (1)

6. form inverted pleat (1) on W.S. (1), oversew in place (1), check equal size of bind on R.S. (1), make sure cut edges are inside the bind (1)

7. tack binding in place (1) flat to garment (1), press (1), check size (1)

8. turn facing to W.S. garment (1), match tailor tacks to buttonhole (1), cut on straight grain (1) through facing (1) slightly larger than hole (1), using needle (1) turn in raw edges (1), hem to binding (1) without stitches showing on R.S. (1), remove tackings, press (1)   40
    —
    50

Answer 50

a. (i) 1. long bell, 2. wrist length bishop, 3. short bell, 4. short puff with band, 5. small cap, 6. short kimono, 7. long high raglan (2 marks for each = 14)
(ii) all set in (1)
(iii) ease at crown, no extra fullness at head (2)   17

b. (i) S.G. arrow (1), notches (2), balance points (3), fitting line (1), lengthening or shortening line (1), position for the easing threads (4)
(ii) back (1) front (1) crown (1)
(iii) opening (1) length (1)   17

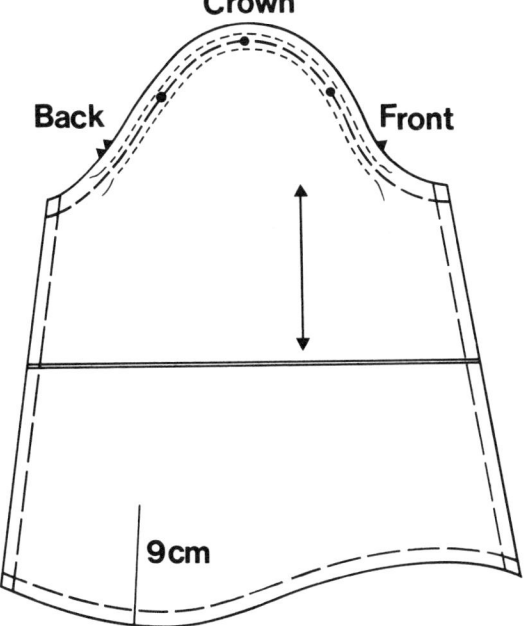

c. (i) sleeve alteration (5)

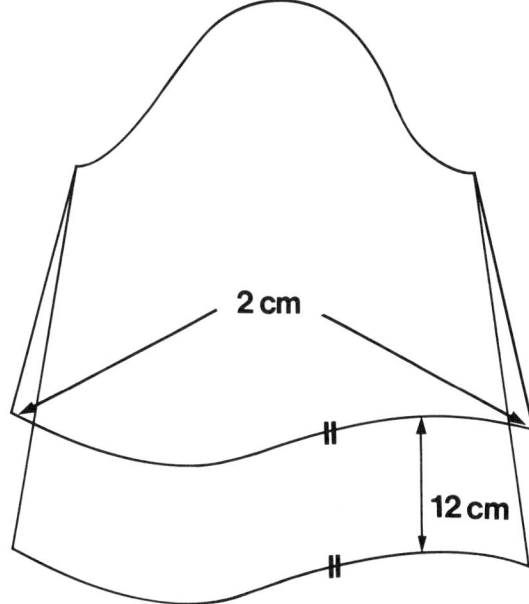

(ii) details of cuff adaptation (4)

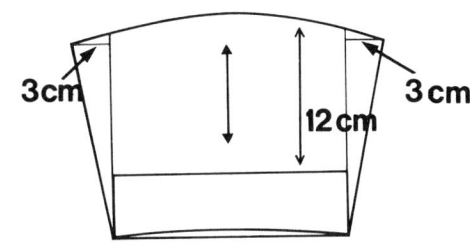

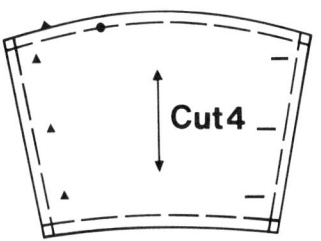

pattern of cuff to show: cut 4, notch, balance point, straight grain, fitting line, position for buttons, position for buttonholes (7)   16

$$\frac{}{50}$$

Answer 51

a. (i) 1. straight cuff with button and buttonhole (4)
2. frill made by elastic in casing (2)
3. plain finish, inconspicuous hem (2)
4. flounced, may be double or neatened with facing or very narrow hem (2)
5. turn back cuff (2)
6. tight fitting, pointed, faced edge and opening (4)
7. ruched, inconspicuous hem (2)

(ii) e.g. 1. shirt-style blouse: cotton poplin
2. nightdress: brushed nylon
3. tailored dress: Crimplene jersey
4. evening dress: nylon chiffon
5. housecoat: Clydella
6. wedding dress: rayon brocade
7. day dress: rayon crêpe
(1 + 1) x 7   32

b.   diagrams (2 marks for each)   6

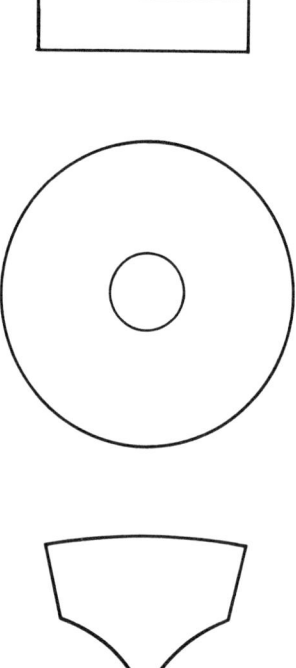

c.   complete edge of sleeve with a narrow hem (1), slip hem (1), machine or hand stitch two rows of gathers to required depth (3), pull up and secure (2), back the gathered section with Paris binding or tape for strength (3), hem tape in place on W.S. of gathering stitches (2)   12
                                                       ─
                                                      50

Answer 52

a.   (i) 1. back, 2. front, 3. front yoke, 4. back yoke, 5. pocket, 6. upper side front (6)
(ii) name (1), description (3), reasons (3)   13

b.   fold marked (1), selvedge marked (1); suitable size for rectangle approximately 10 cm x 6 cm
layout piece number 3 to fold (1)
all other pieces on S.G. (4) (deduct 1 if area of rectangle is too large)   7

c.   (i) name (1), description (3), reasons (3)
(ii) approximately 60 cm (1); estimated by planning a lay on table or newspaper, marking correct width (2)
(iii) binding, 1 card, bias, 1.2 cm wide (4)
zip, 1, skirt weight, 18 cm long (4)
interfacing, 30 cm, suitable for fabric, 80 cm wide (4)
hook and eye, 1, silver, size 2 (4)
thread, 2 reels, suitable for fabric (4)   30
                                                 ─
                                                50

Answer 53

a.   fabric name (1), description (3), reasons (4)   8

b.   (i) tailor tack (1) dot from pattern on F.L.
(1); for exact position (1)
2. reinforce (1) by small machine stitches
(1) close to F.L. (1); for strength (1)
 3. clip to machining (1); to allow give
(1) in turning corner
(ii) loop stitch, overcast or zig-zag together (2)
(iii) to C.F. (1)   12

c.   (i) back shoulder (1); to reduce fullness (1)
(ii) neckline, armhole (1); to prevent
stretch (1)
(iii) neck and armhole facings (1); to prevent rolling to R.S. (1)
(iv) neck facing to zip, neck and armhole
facings to seams (1); to hold firmly (1)
(v) hem (1); invisible (1)   10

d.   (i) 80 cm (1)
(ii) grosgrain (1) 2 or 2.5 cm (1)
(iii) 3.   W.S. together (1) fold in half (1)
lengthwise (1), approximately halfway
down this folded length (1) stitch (1)
4.   bring fold to stitching (1), stitch
through all thicknesses (1), press flat (1)
5.   wrap smaller piece round bow (1)
centring over stitching line (1), turn in
5 mm (1), wrap over other edge (1),
hem in place (1)
(iv) for decoration and to prevent fraying (2)
(v) bows of different fabric from dress, ease
of laundering (2)   20
                    ——
                    50

Answer 54

a.   1. tie belt, 2. patch pocket, 3. buttoned flap,
4. button and buttonhole fastening, 5. fur-
5. trimmed hood, 6. fur-trimmed cuffs, 7. panel
7. seams, 8. set-in sleeve.   8
b.   name of fabric (1), description of fabric (3)   4
c.   (i) suitable, separates to wear with it, colour,
useful addition to wardrobe, fabric quality,
well made, lined, warm, care labelled, shower-
proof, value for money (or other sensible
points up to 10)
(ii) shoulder length, sleeve length, jacket
length, fit over hips, fit at bust, width across
back, comfortable, hood does not fall off (8) 18
d.   comfort, warmth, easy to put on and take
off, strength, longer wear, etc.   5
e.   *method*; test on W.S. of hem, pad on W.S.
sleeve, make sure agent applicator is clean,
use circular motion, work from outside
to inside of stain, allow to dry, check
stain removed, repeat if necessary (7)
agent; Goddard's spray, K2R, Dab-it-off, etc.
(1)   8
f.   A. Woolblend mark, not all pure new wool
(2), B. do not wash (1), C. do not bleach (1),
D. dry clean, all agents suitable (2), E. do not
iron (1)   7
                                                             ──
                                                             50

Answer 55

a.   unpick top stitching without breaking
machine thread, cut off section required, unpick
a little of the seam of the belt, turn in ends, shape
correctly, blind stitch together, press, stitch by
hand to imitate machine top stitching   8
b.   unpick seam, remove all bits of thread, press
flat   3
c.   (i) measure width of belt, add ease and
turnings (3)
(ii) length x breadth and straight
grain along length (3)   6
d.   A1. W.S., A2. machining, A3. raw edges
together (3)
B1. trimmed seam (1) B2. seam pressed open
(1) B3 seam in centre (1), B4. R.S. fabric (1)
B5. section cut away to reduce bulk (2), B6,
raw edges neatened by loop stitch (blanket
stitch) (1)   10
e.   put on coat, fasten, tie belt, pin above and
below belt at both sides of waist on the side
seams, check after removing coat   7
f.   turn in seam allowance (1), pin both ends
(1), check belt fits through (1), fix by hemming
three sides (2), back stitch fourth side (2), finish
off securely (1)   8
g.   remove bits of thread left in, select type and
colour of thread, position, begin with double
back stitch (no knot), six stitches through holes
of button, make large shank, place tie button on
W.S., firm finish on W.S.   8
                                                             ──
                                                             50

Answer 56

a. (i) match notches, match balance marks, underarm seams open and together, yoke seam upwards — vertical pins all round, tack on F.L., fit — try on garment, work on the sleeve side, remove pins and tailor tacks, machine on F.L. from the sleeve side — overlap stitching 4 cm at underarm to strengthen, finish off ends, machine again — not just stitch, finish ends, remove tacking and gathers which show, neaten armhole, detail of how to press (1 mark each)
    (ii) sleeve seam, underarm seam neatening, yoke neatening, shoulder seam neatening (4)   19
b. iron, ironing or sleeve board, pressing cloth   3
c. (i) hot, 200°C, ∗∗∗
    (ii) cool, 100°C, ∗
    (iii) warm, 150°C, ∗∗
    (iv) cool, 100°C, ∗
    (accept any method of heat indication)   4
d. (i) machine, trim, loop stitch or overcast
    (ii) zig-zag and trim
    (iii) bind with bias binding
    (iv) self bind   4
e. open out facing at lower edge, turn up on hemline, tack close to fold, machine seam binding to R.S. of hem, match seams and pin, arrange fullness in darts, tack in position, slip hem and remove tacks, press — fold only, turn facing to W.S. on fold line, slip stitch to hem, press   12
f. needle in (1) out (1) thread (1) ×2
    slip hem (1)   7

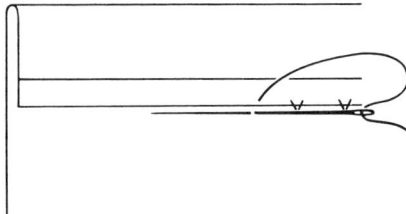 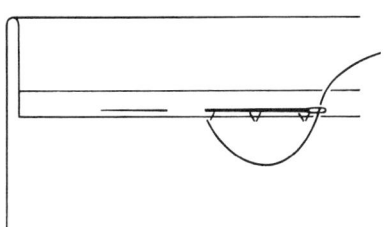

g. neaten edge by machine zig-zag or turn and machine   1
                                                    ―――
                                                    50

Answer 57

a. crease resistance: Tebilized
   shower proof: Silicone
   warmth: Brushed
   flame proof: Proban
   lustre: Mercerized
   bacteria resistance: Acti-fresh
   moth proof: Mitin
   resistance to 'static': Anti-stat
   shrink resistance: Sanforized
   permanently stiff: Trubenized
   (1 mark for each)   10

b. Mitin: wool jersey
   Proban: winceyette, cottons
   Sanforized: poplin, cotton lawn
   Mercerized: cotton poplin
   Trubenized: cotton shirting
   Tebilized: dress-weight rayons, cottons
   Anti-stat: nylon tricot
   Acti-fresh: knitted wool
   Silicone: sailcloth, rayons, cottons
   Brushed: cottons, rayons
   (2 marks for each)   20

c. Mitin: jumper, cardigan
   Proban: nightdress, housecoat
   Sanforized: shirt, jeans
   Mercerized: shirt, blouse
   Trubenized: shirt collar and cuffs
   Tebilized: dress, skirt
   Anti-stat: underskirt, waistslip
   Acti-fresh: socks, vest
   Silicone: anorak, raincoat
   Brushed: pyjamas, dressing gown
   (2 marks for each)   20
                                                       ——
                                                        50

Answer 58

a. name (1), description (3), x 2   8
b. four reasons   4
c. three reasons   3
d. (i) 1. front yoke, 2. back yoke, 3. collar,
   4. front waist band, 5. back waist band, 6.
   pocket, 7. sleeve facing (cuff) (7)
   (ii) piece 2: to fold (1); all other pieces:
   on S.G. (6); piece 4: cut 2 (1)
   (iii) 55–60 cm (2)   17
e. (2 x leg length + hems) + (2 x back length)
   + (sleeve length)   4
f. thread, buttons, zip, interfacing, hook/eye,
   binding ($\frac{1}{2}$ mark for each)   3
g. (i) lengthening and shortening lines (2)
   (ii) darts (2)
   (iii) crutch seam (1)
   (iv) inside leg seam (1)   6

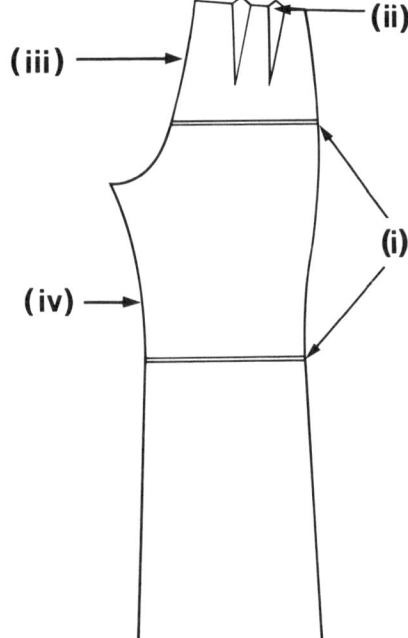

b. (i) sit on chair, measure side waist to chair
   seat, add 2 cm ease (3)
   (ii) use of tape in seam or crossway applied
   to seam after snipping and pressing (2)   5
                                                       ——
                                                        50

Answer 59

a. fitting line: correct size, cutting line: correct
size and good edges, notches: correct positioning,
balance marks: correct positioning, button: position, buttonhole: position, fold line: correct width,
centre back/front: match with trouser seams,
wrap: extension for fastening, vertical lines: side
seam, C.B. and C.F. positions   (1 + 1) x 10   20

b. double stitched seam (1); 1. turning, 2. F.L.,
3. seam allowance trimmed, 4. machining, 5. W.S.,
6 one tow of machining on W.S., 7. back or R.S.
(1 mark for each)   8

c. (i) print patch (1)
     (ii)

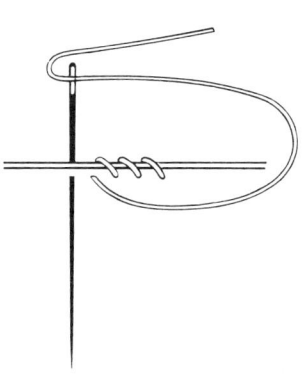 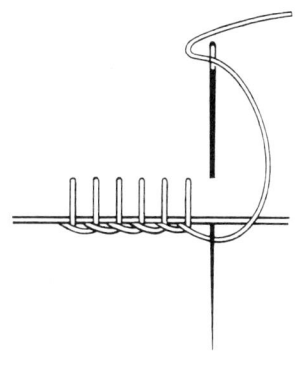

needle in (1)   needle in (1)
needle out (1)   needle out (1)
thread in relation   thread in relation to
to needle (1)   needle (1)
oversewing (1)   loop or blanket stitch (1)
(iii) iron-on motif, or similar — detail
of iron heat, etc. (4)   13

d. work section by section thus enabling the
garment to be made up more quickly and making
it easier to handle during construction (3)
pocket, collar, sleeve, yokes to bodice, waistband,
front band (correct order not essential here) (6)   9
                                      ——
                                      50

Answer 60

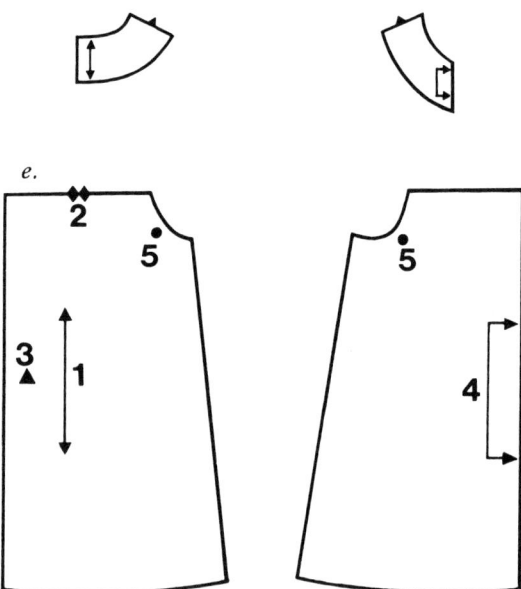

d.

8

e.

a. *sketches*

front: high neck (1), yoke (1), armhole ruffle (1), gathers (1), armhole seam (1), shape of garment (2)

back: ruffle (1), gathers (1), C.B. seam (1), zip (1), neck (1), armhole seam (1), yoke (1), shape of garment (1) 15

b. 1. front, 2, front yoke, 3. back, 4. back yoke, 5. front neck facing, 6. back neck facing, 7. armhole ruffle, 8. armhole facing (1 mark each) 8

c. cut one piece, binding hem edge or narrow hem machined, alternatively cut two half-pieces up to selvedge 2

correct placement on tracings (6)
names (1 for each)
1. straight grain
2. notches
3. zip length
4. place to fold
5. balance mark 11

f. 1. where to sew, 2. where to cut, 3. position of zip 3

g. garment view, size, fabric width 3

———
50

Answer 61

a.   double, single, reinforced, raw, stay, neatened, sewn, after, loops, shank, between, button, fabric, flat, button, fastened, moulded, button, made, sewing, thicker, longer, sewn, single, colour, thickness   26

b.   (i) A. tweed, flannel, etc.: double-breasted coat, for decorative button; B. poplin, printed cotton etc.: C.F. dress or blouse, for decorative button (4)
(ii) tape, bias binding, Paris binding, fabric, ribbon, interfacing (5)   9

c.   C1. fold edge, C2. C.F. lines together, C3. pin to mark position, C4. R.S. R front, C5. buttonhole horizontal, C6. facing (1 mark for each (6))

d.   D7. machining (1), D8. pin (1) through centre (1) of buttonhole, D9. fold, edge of opening (1), D10. C.F. line (1), D11. W.S. fabric (1), D12. R.S. fabric (1), D13. vertical buttonhole (1), D14. edge neatening (1)   15
                                                                     ——
                                                                     50

Answer 62

a.   buttonhole C: horizontal, one square and one round end, strain at round end, end of buttonhole 3 mm over the C.F. to allow button to be on C.F.
buttonhole D: vertical, two square ends, no strain, to be on C.F. and in centre of strap   6

b.   (i) box pleat opening (1); fold to R.S. on fold line (1), edge tack (1), match centres (1), turn 3 mm (1) to R.S. (1) on free edge (1), press (1), tack in place (1), check folds on either side of C.F. are equal (2), machine close to fold through two layers (1), machine close to fold through three layers (2), remove tacks and press (2)
(ii) poplin, gingham, afgalaine, etc.; R.S. and W.S. must be alike (3)   19

c.

d.   not, washing, corners, weak, fray, frequently, single, neatened, wrong, facing, early, garment, before, facing, seam   15
                                                                     ——
                                                                     50

Answer 63

a.   1 set in sleeve, 2 bust dart, 3 neckband, 4. C.F. opening fastened with button and buttonholes, 5 shaped slits, 6 wide sleeve bottom bottom (1 mark for each)   6

b.   continuous wrap (strip)   1

c.   nape to hem x 2 + hems
        60 cm x 2 + 10 cm   = 130 cm
  length of sleeve x 2
        70 cm x 2   = 140 cm (5)
    Amount required   = 2.70 m (2)
                                  7

d.   name of fabric (1), description (3), reasons (4)   8

e.   braid type relating to fabric chosen (1), width not more than 5 cm (1)   2

f.   mitre braid on W.S. by making darts, centre dart tapers to nothing at C.F. of braid, two equal darts equidistant from the centre, darts stitched and pressed open   4

g.   (i) use single thread, colour to match, begin firmly, no knot, use match to form shank, sew over six times, remove match, wrap thread round to form shank (8)
(ii) W.S. should have bar tack (1), loop stitch threads together neatly (1); diagram (2) 12

h.   (i) neck band: 1 round end and 1 square end, round end to opening to take strain C.F.: both ends will be the same, no pull (4)

(ii)

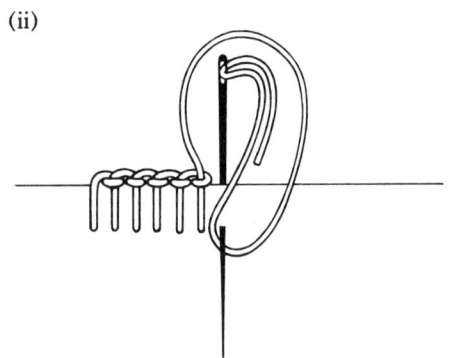

    needle in (1), needle out (1), position of needle in relation to last stitch (1), thread round needle (1), thread from last stitch (1), edge indicated (1)   10
                              —
                            50

Answer 64

a.   facing, lining, reduce (3)
Diagram A   R.S., facing, R.S., tack, fitting, line, clip, curve (8)
Diagram B   position, underlay, tacking (3)
Diagram C   facing, W.S., seam, W.S., tack, top, tacking, press, right, faced, underlay, fitting, line, tack (14)
Diagram D   W.S., pin, underlay, facing, flat, fitting, line, tacking (8)
Diagram E   seam allowances, 1 cm, neaten, blanket (loop) (5)   41

b.   (i) fabric type stated must be suitable, e.g. afgalaine (1)
(ii) e.g. gaberdine   zig-zag machining
           tweed   binding
           serge   overcasting   (6)
(iii) e.g. tricel, rayon satin   (2)   9
                              —
                            50

Answer 65

a.   1 square neckline (2), 2 side front button and buttonhole fastening (3), 3 R.S. faced neckline (3), 4 plain short sleeve, set-in (2), 5 small fitted turned-back cuff (3)   13

b.   printed: pattern on R.S. darker than on W.S. (3)
Tricelon: mixture of tricel and Celon (3)
pongee: woven, plain weave, textured yarn — similar to shantung (2)   8

c.   (i) e.g. organdie (1); neckline, opening, cuff (3)
(ii) 5 buttons, 2 cm diameter with shank, to match fabric (5), 1 reel of Drima to match fabric (3), 1 hook, silver, size 00 (4)   16

d.   (i) square neck, front opening (2); reasons (2)
(ii) sleeve to cap sleeve or sleeveless, lengthen and add flare to skirt (2); reasons (2)
(iii) fabric (1); reasons (4)   13
                              —
                            50

Answer 66

a.   1. large pointed turned-back cuff (3), 2. sleeve pleated into cuff (2), 3. flat pointed collar (3), 4. gathered sleeve head (2), 5. embroidered motif (appliqué) (2) 6. darted to fit waist (2), 7. C.F. button and buttonhole fastening (2)   16

b.   tricel: tri-acetate rayon (2)
    georgette: plain weave, crêpe yarn, crinkly appearance, self-coloured (4)   6

c.   (i) copy of part of motif (1); three stitches: named (3), drawn (3), threads (2), colour(s) (1)
    (ii) crewel: size 8/9 (2)
    (iii) stitch diagrams: needle in (1), needle out (1), thread action (1), finished stitch (1)
    x 2   20

d.   shadow, smaller, shape, leaves, stem/back, closed herringbone, wrong.   8
                              —
                             50

d.   (i) shaped facing, crossway facing (2)
    (ii) 1.   one layer cuff (1): machine (1) to W.S. sleeve (1), turn in other on F.L. (1), hem into machining (1).
    2.   both layers of cuff (1): machine on F.L. (1) to W.S. sleeve (1), neaten with zig-zag (1) press to R.S. and catch stitch edges of cuff together for 2 cm (1)   12

e.   collar: shape of curve (1), joining original lines (2)
    sleeve: add width — 5 cm (1) at both sides (1) shorten length (1), curve base (1), shape of curve (1)
    band: line parallel to straight edge (1), not too wide to give 3 cm (1)   10
                                —
                             50

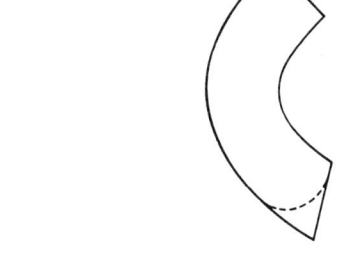

Answer 67

a.   back, front, collar, sleeve, cuff   5

b.   1. separate pattern pieces (1), 2. sort out those required (1), 3. press if crumpled (1), 4. check size and adjust if necessary (1), 5. prepare fabric (1), 6. plan lay (1), 7. pin on pattern pieces (1), 8. cut out (1)   8

c.   back: shoulder dart, waist dart, sleeve balance point, C.B. (4)
    front: fold or C.F., buttonholes, waist dart, sleeve balance point (4)
    sleeve: crown, front balance point, back balance point, pleat positions (4)
    collar: C.B., shoulder (2)
    cuff: underarm seam (1)   15

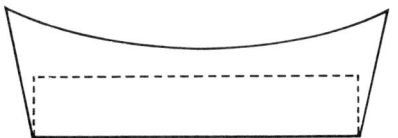

Answer 68

a. 1. ribbon on sleeve to fit arm (2), 2. full raglan sleeve – short (3), 3. faggotting on raglan seam (2), 4. low round gathered neckline (3), 5. shirring at waistline (wide band) (3), 6. frilled blouse hemline (2)   15

b. fine, soft, absorbent, washes well, hardwearing, gathers easily, drip dry   7

c. 6. make narrow hems (1) on edge of sleeve (1) and on edge of bodice (1)
2. slip hem (1) in place; press (1)
1. use long and short tacking (1) to hold sleeve edge (1) in position on
7. thick paper or thin card (1)
4. place finished edge (1) of bodice (1) 5 mm (1) away
5. from sleeve edge (1), parallel and tack carefully (2)
3. twisted (1) faggot together (1) (7 for correct order and 16 for detail)   23

d. 1. thread out (1), needle in (1)
2. needle in (1), needle out (1), thread (1)   5
—
50

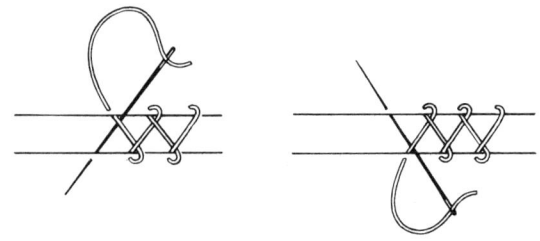

Answer 69

a. 1. low V neckline (1), 2. large bow from collar (2), 3. bishop sleeve (1), 4. fitted cuff with large buttonhole (2)   6

b. small geometric pattern (1) woven (1) into fabric, soft (1) lightweight (1) R.S. and W.S. alike (1), all self-colour pattern (1), rayon fibres used in crêpe weave (2)   8

c. (i) bodice front, bodice back, sleeve, <u>cuff</u>, <u>collar/tie</u> (5)
(ii) see underlinings above (2)   7

d. (i) French: wears well
(ii) bound/continuous strip: strong
(iii) self bind: comfortable
(iv) machined: fabric frays easily (4 + 4)   8

e. 1. remove pattern, 2. separate pieces, 3. tack main sections together, 4. try on, 5. work shoulder seam and work underarm seams (bodice), 6. press, 7. make collar/tie, 8. attach collar, 9. work sleeve opening, 10. work sleeve seam, 11. gather sleeve head, 12. gather wrist, 13. make cuff, 14. attach cuff, 15. set in sleeve, 16. try on, 17. neaten armhole, 18. work hem, 19. work buttonholes on cuffs, 20. attach buttons, 21. final press   21
—
50

Answer 70

a. length (1), fastening (1), waist finish (1), fullness (1), other details e.g. frill, yoke, pocket, etc. (1½)   5½

b. disco, party, shopping, work, etc. (1)   1

c. beads, bangle, ear-rings, shoes/clogs, rings, tank-top, etc. – expect at least two (1) and description (2) x 2   6
—
4 x 12½
50

Index

The figures refer to question numbers.